# MY JOURNAL OF FARTS
## by

_____

# FART GLOSSARY

**Amplified Fart:** A regular fart done on a metal or hollow surface (like bleachers) will have an exaggerated sound & cool echo.

**Command Fart:** A fart which can be held in until just the right moment and provide a grand exit from a room upon command.

**Cushioned Fart:** When a fart is allowed to escape but the butt is strategically pushed down into a soft surface, hoping it will mask all sound and smell until passed. Useful during office meetings or public events.

**Organic Fart:** A fart by a health food obsessed person who has eaten too much fiber and is proud of their excess gas and uses it as an opportunity to tell you about their natural diet.

**Splatter Fart:** Oops... you didn't see that one coming.

**Squeaker Fart:** Anticipating that you have a giant thunder rumble on the way, you release the butt cheeks just a little to allow a small amount of gas to escape and either delay or minimize the huge one on the way.

**Balloon Fart:** This one is identical to a deflating balloon and is made up of a series of smaller farts which may last an embarrassingly long amount of time. The small scents can combine for a massive stink factor.

**Involuntary Fart:** You didn't even feel the urge to pass gas but a tiny toot escapes and it's usually followed by a quick throat clearing cough as cover.

**Silent But Deadly Fart:** The key to this one is that nobody hears anything, but the deadly stench soon suffocates anyone within breathing distance.

**Sleeper Fart:** Anybody who insists they don't fart will hold it in all day long to prove their point, but when they fall asleep, their body decides it's time to release all of that pressure and it's loud, long and smelly.

**Shower Fart:** Farts don't smell good as it is, but release one in the shower and that nasty stench will be stuck in your nose for days. Ugh.

# A FART BY ANY OTHER NAME...

Enjoy this list of alternative phrases from around the world to describe farts.

| | |
|---|---|
| After Dinner Mint | Cleft A Boofer |
| Air Poop | Colon Bowlin' |
| Anal Salute | Cut The Cheese |
| Backdoor Trumpet | Heiny Burp |
| Bakin' Brownies | Let A Beefer |
| Blow Chocolate Kisses | Poopski |
| Bottom Burp | Rear Roar |
| Breaking Wind | Pants Sneeze |
| Brown Haze | Split The Seam |
| Butt Yodeling | Strip A Gear |
| Butt Cheek Squeak | Toot Your Horn |
| Buttock Bassoon | Back Blast |
| Butt Burping | Barking Spider |
| Carpet Creeper | Booty Belch |
| Extreme Fumagatory Essence | Colonic Calliope |
| Fanny Bubble | Death Breath |
| Fire In The Hole | Release The Foghorn |
| Morning Thunder | Fumigator |
| Mudslapper | Jockey Burner |
| Poopy Tunes | Who Let The Beans Out |
| Puffer | Odor Bubble |
| Rectal Turbulence | Panty Burp |
| Ripsnorter | Pop A Fluffie |
| Scented Scream | Rump Ripper |
| Stink Sliders | Stink Burger |
| Sphincter Whistle | Tushy Tickle |
| Thunder Buns | Turd Tremor |
| Trouser Cough | Lethal Cloud |
| Tooshie Belch | Turd Grumble |

**Date:** ___ / ___ / ___     Sun  Mon  Tue  Wed  Thu  Fri  Sat

**Time of Fart:** _____ am/pm     **Duration:** ___ min ___ sec

**Fart Intensity:**
- ○ **Gentle Puff** (barely there, quick & unscented)
- ○ **SBD** (silent but deadly)
- ○ **Military March** (series of puffs with mild scent)
- ○ **Classic** (quick, loud, stinky scent but fades quickly)
- ○ **Thunder Rumble** (long, loud & stinky)
- ○ **Diarrhea Storm** (explosive, wet & clears the room)
- ○ **Oh, Crap!** (self explanatory)

**Fart Enjoyment Scale:**  ☺ ☺ ☺ ☺ ☺

**Who Noticed:** _____

**Who Left The Room:** _____

---

**Date:** ___ / ___ / ___     Sun  Mon  Tue  Wed  Thu  Fri  Sat

**Time of Fart:** _____ am/pm     **Duration:** ___ min ___ sec

**Fart Intensity:**
- ○ **Gentle Puff** (barely there, quick & unscented)
- ○ **SBD** (silent but deadly)
- ○ **Military March** (series of puffs with mild scent)
- ○ **Classic** (quick, loud, stinky scent but fades quickly)
- ○ **Thunder Rumble** (long, loud & stinky)
- ○ **Diarrhea Storm** (explosive, wet & clears the room)
- ○ **Oh, Crap!** (self explanatory)

**Fart Enjoyment Scale:**  ☺ ☺ ☺ ☺ ☺

**Who Noticed:** _____

**Who Left The Room:** _____

# NOTES

# NOTES

**Date:** ___ / ___ / ___    Sun  Mon  Tue  Wed  Thu  Fri  Sat

**Time of Fart:** _____ am/pm    **Duration:** ___ min ___ sec

**Fart Intensity:**
- ○ **Gentle Puff** (barely there, quick & unscented)
- ○ **SBD** (silent but deadly)
- ○ **Military March** (series of puffs with mild scent)
- ○ **Classic** (quick, loud, stinky scent but fades quickly)
- ○ **Thunder Rumble** (long, loud & stinky)
- ○ **Diarrhea Storm** (explosive, wet & clears the room)
- ○ **Oh, Crap!** (self explanatory)

**Fart Enjoyment Scale:**  ☺ ☺ ☺ ☺ ☺

**Who Noticed:** _____

**Who Left The Room:** _____

---

**Date:** ___ / ___ / ___    Sun  Mon  Tue  Wed  Thu  Fri  Sat

**Time of Fart:** _____ am/pm    **Duration:** ___ min ___ sec

**Fart Intensity:**
- ○ **Gentle Puff** (barely there, quick & unscented)
- ○ **SBD** (silent but deadly)
- ○ **Military March** (series of puffs with mild scent)
- ○ **Classic** (quick, loud, stinky scent but fades quickly)
- ○ **Thunder Rumble** (long, loud & stinky)
- ○ **Diarrhea Storm** (explosive, wet & clears the room)
- ○ **Oh, Crap!** (self explanatory)

**Fart Enjoyment Scale:**  ☺ ☺ ☺ ☺ ☺

**Who Noticed:** _____

**Who Left The Room:** _____

# NOTES

_____

_____

_____

_____

_____

_____

_____

_____

_____

_____

_____

# NOTES

_____

_____

_____

_____

_____

_____

_____

_____

_____

**Date:** ___ / ___ / ___    Sun  Mon  Tue  Wed  Thu  Fri  Sat

**Time of Fart:** _____ am/pm    **Duration:** ___ min ___ sec

**Fart Intensity:**

- ○ **Gentle Puff** (barely there, quick & unscented)
- ○ **SBD** (silent but deadly)
- ○ **Military March** (series of puffs with mild scent)
- ○ **Classic** (quick, loud, stinky scent but fades quickly)
- ○ **Thunder Rumble** (long, loud & stinky)
- ○ **Diarrhea Storm** (explosive, wet & clears the room)
- ○ **Oh, Crap!** (self explanatory)

**Fart Enjoyment Scale:**  ☺ ☺ ☺ ☺ ☺

**Who Noticed:** _____

**Who Left The Room:** _____

---

**Date:** ___ / ___ / ___    Sun  Mon  Tue  Wed  Thu  Fri  Sat

**Time of Fart:** _____ am/pm    **Duration:** ___ min ___ sec

**Fart Intensity:**

- ○ **Gentle Puff** (barely there, quick & unscented)
- ○ **SBD** (silent but deadly)
- ○ **Military March** (series of puffs with mild scent)
- ○ **Classic** (quick, loud, stinky scent but fades quickly)
- ○ **Thunder Rumble** (long, loud & stinky)
- ○ **Diarrhea Storm** (explosive, wet & clears the room)
- ○ **Oh, Crap!** (self explanatory)

**Fart Enjoyment Scale:**  ☺ ☺ ☺ ☺ ☺

**Who Noticed:** _____

**Who Left The Room:** _____

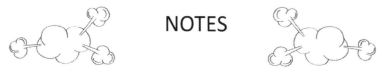

# NOTES

---
---
---
---
---
---
---
---
---
---
---
---

# NOTES

---
---
---
---
---
---
---
---
---

**Date:** ___ / ___ / ___     Sun   Mon   Tue   Wed   Thu   Fri   Sat

**Time of Fart:** _____ am/pm     **Duration:** ___ min ___ sec

**Fart Intensity:**
- ○ **Gentle Puff** (barely there, quick & unscented)
- ○ **SBD** (silent but deadly)
- ○ **Military March** (series of puffs with mild scent)
- ○ **Classic** (quick, loud, stinky scent but fades quickly)
- ○ **Thunder Rumble** (long, loud & stinky)
- ○ **Diarrhea Storm** (explosive, wet & clears the room)
- ○ **Oh, Crap!** (self explanatory)

**Fart Enjoyment Scale:**  ☺ ☺ ☺ ☺ ☺

**Who Noticed:** _____

**Who Left The Room:** _____

---

**Date:** ___ / ___ / ___     Sun   Mon   Tue   Wed   Thu   Fri   Sat

**Time of Fart:** _____ am/pm     **Duration:** ___ min ___ sec

**Fart Intensity:**
- ○ **Gentle Puff** (barely there, quick & unscented)
- ○ **SBD** (silent but deadly)
- ○ **Military March** (series of puffs with mild scent)
- ○ **Classic** (quick, loud, stinky scent but fades quickly)
- ○ **Thunder Rumble** (long, loud & stinky)
- ○ **Diarrhea Storm** (explosive, wet & clears the room)
- ○ **Oh, Crap!** (self explanatory)

**Fart Enjoyment Scale:**  ☺ ☺ ☺ ☺ ☺

**Who Noticed:** _____

**Who Left The Room:** _____

# NOTES

---

## NOTES

**Date:** ___ / ___ / ___    Sun  Mon  Tue  Wed  Thu  Fri  Sat

**Time of Fart:** _____ am/pm    **Duration:** ___ min ___ sec

**Fart Intensity:**
- ○ **Gentle Puff** (barely there, quick & unscented)
- ○ **SBD** (silent but deadly)
- ○ **Military March** (series of puffs with mild scent)
- ○ **Classic** (quick, loud, stinky scent but fades quickly)
- ○ **Thunder Rumble** (long, loud & stinky)
- ○ **Diarrhea Storm** (explosive, wet & clears the room)
- ○ **Oh, Crap!** (self explanatory)

**Fart Enjoyment Scale:**  ☺ ☺ ☺ ☺ ☺

**Who Noticed:** _____

**Who Left The Room:** _____

---

**Date:** ___ / ___ / ___    Sun  Mon  Tue  Wed  Thu  Fri  Sat

**Time of Fart:** _____ am/pm    **Duration:** ___ min ___ sec

**Fart Intensity:**
- ○ **Gentle Puff** (barely there, quick & unscented)
- ○ **SBD** (silent but deadly)
- ○ **Military March** (series of puffs with mild scent)
- ○ **Classic** (quick, loud, stinky scent but fades quickly)
- ○ **Thunder Rumble** (long, loud & stinky)
- ○ **Diarrhea Storm** (explosive, wet & clears the room)
- ○ **Oh, Crap!** (self explanatory)

**Fart Enjoyment Scale:**  ☺ ☺ ☺ ☺ ☺

**Who Noticed:** _____

**Who Left The Room:** _____

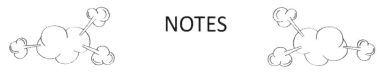

# NOTES

_____

_____

_____

_____

_____

_____

_____

_____

_____

_____

# NOTES

_____

_____

_____

_____

_____

_____

_____

_____

_____

_____

**Date:** ___ / ___ / ___    Sun  Mon  Tue  Wed  Thu  Fri  Sat

**Time of Fart:** _____ am/pm    **Duration:** ___ min ___ sec

**Fart Intensity:**
- ○ **Gentle Puff** (barely there, quick & unscented)
- ○ **SBD** (silent but deadly)
- ○ **Military March** (series of puffs with mild scent)
- ○ **Classic** (quick, loud, stinky scent but fades quickly)
- ○ **Thunder Rumble** (long, loud & stinky)
- ○ **Diarrhea Storm** (explosive, wet & clears the room)
- ○ **Oh, Crap!** (self explanatory)

**Fart Enjoyment Scale:** ☺ ☺ ☺ ☺ ☺

**Who Noticed:** _____

**Who Left The Room:** _____

---

**Date:** ___ / ___ / ___    Sun  Mon  Tue  Wed  Thu  Fri  Sat

**Time of Fart:** _____ am/pm    **Duration:** ___ min ___ sec

**Fart Intensity:**
- ○ **Gentle Puff** (barely there, quick & unscented)
- ○ **SBD** (silent but deadly)
- ○ **Military March** (series of puffs with mild scent)
- ○ **Classic** (quick, loud, stinky scent but fades quickly)
- ○ **Thunder Rumble** (long, loud & stinky)
- ○ **Diarrhea Storm** (explosive, wet & clears the room)
- ○ **Oh, Crap!** (self explanatory)

**Fart Enjoyment Scale:** ☺ ☺ ☺ ☺ ☺

**Who Noticed:** _____

**Who Left The Room:** _____

# NOTES

---

---

---

---

---

---

---

---

---

---

---

---

# NOTES

---

---

---

---

---

---

---

---

---

**Date:** ___ / ___ / ___    Sun  Mon  Tue  Wed  Thu  Fri  Sat

**Time of Fart:** _____ am/pm    **Duration:** ___ min ___ sec

**Fart Intensity:**
- ○ **Gentle Puff** (barely there, quick & unscented)
- ○ **SBD** (silent but deadly)
- ○ **Military March** (series of puffs with mild scent)
- ○ **Classic** (quick, loud, stinky scent but fades quickly)
- ○ **Thunder Rumble** (long, loud & stinky)
- ○ **Diarrhea Storm** (explosive, wet & clears the room)
- ○ **Oh, Crap!** (self explanatory)

**Fart Enjoyment Scale:** 😊 😊 😊 😊 😊

**Who Noticed:** _____

**Who Left The Room:** _____

---

**Date:** ___ / ___ / ___    Sun  Mon  Tue  Wed  Thu  Fri  Sat

**Time of Fart:** _____ am/pm    **Duration:** ___ min ___ sec

**Fart Intensity:**
- ○ **Gentle Puff** (barely there, quick & unscented)
- ○ **SBD** (silent but deadly)
- ○ **Military March** (series of puffs with mild scent)
- ○ **Classic** (quick, loud, stinky scent but fades quickly)
- ○ **Thunder Rumble** (long, loud & stinky)
- ○ **Diarrhea Storm** (explosive, wet & clears the room)
- ○ **Oh, Crap!** (self explanatory)

**Fart Enjoyment Scale:** 😊 😊 😊 😊 😊

**Who Noticed:** _____

**Who Left The Room:** _____

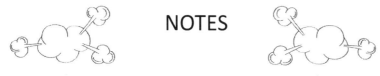

# NOTES

_____

_____

_____

_____

_____

_____

_____

_____

_____

_____

_____

_____

# NOTES

_____

_____

_____

_____

_____

_____

_____

_____

_____

**Date:** ___ / ___ / ___     Sun  Mon  Tue  Wed  Thu  Fri  Sat

**Time of Fart:** _____ am/pm     **Duration:** ___ min ___ sec

**Fart Intensity:**
- ○ **Gentle Puff** (barely there, quick & unscented)
- ○ **SBD** (silent but deadly)
- ○ **Military March** (series of puffs with mild scent)
- ○ **Classic** (quick, loud, stinky scent but fades quickly)
- ○ **Thunder Rumble** (long, loud & stinky)
- ○ **Diarrhea Storm** (explosive, wet & clears the room)
- ○ **Oh, Crap!** (self explanatory)

**Fart Enjoyment Scale:** 😊 😊 😊 😊 😊

**Who Noticed:** _____

**Who Left The Room:** _____

---

**Date:** ___ / ___ / ___     Sun  Mon  Tue  Wed  Thu  Fri  Sat

**Time of Fart:** _____ am/pm     **Duration:** ___ min ___ sec

**Fart Intensity:**
- ○ **Gentle Puff** (barely there, quick & unscented)
- ○ **SBD** (silent but deadly)
- ○ **Military March** (series of puffs with mild scent)
- ○ **Classic** (quick, loud, stinky scent but fades quickly)
- ○ **Thunder Rumble** (long, loud & stinky)
- ○ **Diarrhea Storm** (explosive, wet & clears the room)
- ○ **Oh, Crap!** (self explanatory)

**Fart Enjoyment Scale:** 😊 😊 😊 😊 😊

**Who Noticed:** _____

**Who Left The Room:** _____

# NOTES

_____

_____

_____

_____

_____

_____

_____

_____

_____

_____

_____

_____

# NOTES

_____

_____

_____

_____

_____

_____

_____

_____

_____

**Date:** ___ / ___ / ___     Sun  Mon  Tue  Wed  Thu  Fri  Sat

**Time of Fart:** _____ am/pm     **Duration:** ___ min ___ sec

**Fart Intensity:**
- ○ **Gentle Puff** (barely there, quick & unscented)
- ○ **SBD** (silent but deadly)
- ○ **Military March** (series of puffs with mild scent)
- ○ **Classic** (quick, loud, stinky scent but fades quickly)
- ○ **Thunder Rumble** (long, loud & stinky)
- ○ **Diarrhea Storm** (explosive, wet & clears the room)
- ○ **Oh, Crap!** (self explanatory)

**Fart Enjoyment Scale:** ☺ ☺ ☺ ☺ ☺

**Who Noticed:** _____

**Who Left The Room:** _____

---

**Date:** ___ / ___ / ___     Sun  Mon  Tue  Wed  Thu  Fri  Sat

**Time of Fart:** _____ am/pm     **Duration:** ___ min ___ sec

**Fart Intensity:**
- ○ **Gentle Puff** (barely there, quick & unscented)
- ○ **SBD** (silent but deadly)
- ○ **Military March** (series of puffs with mild scent)
- ○ **Classic** (quick, loud, stinky scent but fades quickly)
- ○ **Thunder Rumble** (long, loud & stinky)
- ○ **Diarrhea Storm** (explosive, wet & clears the room)
- ○ **Oh, Crap!** (self explanatory)

**Fart Enjoyment Scale:** ☺ ☺ ☺ ☺ ☺

**Who Noticed:** _____

**Who Left The Room:** _____

# NOTES

_____

_____

_____

_____

_____

_____

_____

_____

_____

_____

_____

# NOTES

_____

_____

_____

_____

_____

_____

_____

_____

_____

**Date:** ___ / ___ / ___    Sun   Mon   Tue   Wed   Thu   Fri   Sat

**Time of Fart:** _____ am/pm    **Duration:** ___ min ___ sec

**Fart Intensity:**
- ○ **Gentle Puff** (barely there, quick & unscented)
- ○ **SBD** (silent but deadly)
- ○ **Military March** (series of puffs with mild scent)
- ○ **Classic** (quick, loud, stinky scent but fades quickly)
- ○ **Thunder Rumble** (long, loud & stinky)
- ○ **Diarrhea Storm** (explosive, wet & clears the room)
- ○ **Oh, Crap!** (self explanatory)

**Fart Enjoyment Scale:** ☺ ☺ ☺ ☺ ☺

**Who Noticed:** _____

**Who Left The Room:** _____

---

**Date:** ___ / ___ / ___    Sun   Mon   Tue   Wed   Thu   Fri   Sat

**Time of Fart:** _____ am/pm    **Duration:** ___ min ___ sec

**Fart Intensity:**
- ○ **Gentle Puff** (barely there, quick & unscented)
- ○ **SBD** (silent but deadly)
- ○ **Military March** (series of puffs with mild scent)
- ○ **Classic** (quick, loud, stinky scent but fades quickly)
- ○ **Thunder Rumble** (long, loud & stinky)
- ○ **Diarrhea Storm** (explosive, wet & clears the room)
- ○ **Oh, Crap!** (self explanatory)

**Fart Enjoyment Scale:** ☺ ☺ ☺ ☺ ☺

**Who Noticed:** _____

**Who Left The Room:** _____

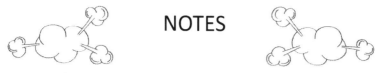

# NOTES

_____
_____
_____
_____
_____
_____
_____
_____
_____
_____
_____
_____

# NOTES

_____
_____
_____
_____
_____
_____
_____
_____
_____

**Date:** ___ / ___ / ___     Sun  Mon  Tue  Wed  Thu  Fri  Sat

**Time of Fart:** _____ am/pm     **Duration:** ___ min ___ sec

**Fart Intensity:**
- ○ **Gentle Puff** (barely there, quick & unscented)
- ○ **SBD** (silent but deadly)
- ○ **Military March** (series of puffs with mild scent)
- ○ **Classic** (quick, loud, stinky scent but fades quickly)
- ○ **Thunder Rumble** (long, loud & stinky)
- ○ **Diarrhea Storm** (explosive, wet & clears the room)
- ○ **Oh, Crap!** (self explanatory)

**Fart Enjoyment Scale:**  ☺ ☺ ☺ ☺ ☺

**Who Noticed:** _____

**Who Left The Room:** _____

---

**Date:** ___ / ___ / ___     Sun  Mon  Tue  Wed  Thu  Fri  Sat

**Time of Fart:** _____ am/pm     **Duration:** ___ min ___ sec

**Fart Intensity:**
- ○ **Gentle Puff** (barely there, quick & unscented)
- ○ **SBD** (silent but deadly)
- ○ **Military March** (series of puffs with mild scent)
- ○ **Classic** (quick, loud, stinky scent but fades quickly)
- ○ **Thunder Rumble** (long, loud & stinky)
- ○ **Diarrhea Storm** (explosive, wet & clears the room)
- ○ **Oh, Crap!** (self explanatory)

**Fart Enjoyment Scale:**  ☺ ☺ ☺ ☺ ☺

**Who Noticed:** _____

**Who Left The Room:** _____

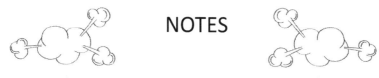

# NOTES

_____

_____

_____

_____

_____

_____

_____

_____

_____

_____

_____

_____

# NOTES

_____

_____

_____

_____

_____

_____

_____

_____

_____

_____

**Date:** ___ / ___ / ___     Sun  Mon  Tue  Wed  Thu  Fri  Sat

**Time of Fart:** _____ am/pm     **Duration:** ___ min ___ sec

**Fart Intensity:**
- ○ **Gentle Puff** (barely there, quick & unscented)
- ○ **SBD** (silent but deadly)
- ○ **Military March** (series of puffs with mild scent)
- ○ **Classic** (quick, loud, stinky scent but fades quickly)
- ○ **Thunder Rumble** (long, loud & stinky)
- ○ **Diarrhea Storm** (explosive, wet & clears the room)
- ○ **Oh, Crap!** (self explanatory)

**Fart Enjoyment Scale:** ☺ ☺ ☺ ☺ ☺

**Who Noticed:** _____

**Who Left The Room:** _____

---

**Date:** ___ / ___ / ___     Sun  Mon  Tue  Wed  Thu  Fri  Sat

**Time of Fart:** _____ am/pm     **Duration:** ___ min ___ sec

**Fart Intensity:**
- ○ **Gentle Puff** (barely there, quick & unscented)
- ○ **SBD** (silent but deadly)
- ○ **Military March** (series of puffs with mild scent)
- ○ **Classic** (quick, loud, stinky scent but fades quickly)
- ○ **Thunder Rumble** (long, loud & stinky)
- ○ **Diarrhea Storm** (explosive, wet & clears the room)
- ○ **Oh, Crap!** (self explanatory)

**Fart Enjoyment Scale:** ☺ ☺ ☺ ☺ ☺

**Who Noticed:** _____

**Who Left The Room:** _____

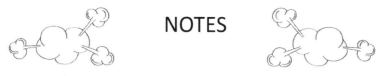

# NOTES

_____

_____

_____

_____

_____

_____

_____

_____

_____

_____

_____

# NOTES

_____

_____

_____

_____

_____

_____

_____

_____

_____

**Date:** ___ / ___ / ___     Sun  Mon  Tue  Wed  Thu  Fri  Sat

**Time of Fart:** _____ am/pm     **Duration:** ___ min ___ sec

**Fart Intensity:**
- ○ **Gentle Puff** (barely there, quick & unscented)
- ○ **SBD** (silent but deadly)
- ○ **Military March** (series of puffs with mild scent)
- ○ **Classic** (quick, loud, stinky scent but fades quickly)
- ○ **Thunder Rumble** (long, loud & stinky)
- ○ **Diarrhea Storm** (explosive, wet & clears the room)
- ○ **Oh, Crap!** (self explanatory)

**Fart Enjoyment Scale:** ☺ ☺ ☺ ☺ ☺

**Who Noticed:** _____

**Who Left The Room:** _____

---

**Date:** ___ / ___ / ___     Sun  Mon  Tue  Wed  Thu  Fri  Sat

**Time of Fart:** _____ am/pm     **Duration:** ___ min ___ sec

**Fart Intensity:**
- ○ **Gentle Puff** (barely there, quick & unscented)
- ○ **SBD** (silent but deadly)
- ○ **Military March** (series of puffs with mild scent)
- ○ **Classic** (quick, loud, stinky scent but fades quickly)
- ○ **Thunder Rumble** (long, loud & stinky)
- ○ **Diarrhea Storm** (explosive, wet & clears the room)
- ○ **Oh, Crap!** (self explanatory)

**Fart Enjoyment Scale:** ☺ ☺ ☺ ☺ ☺

**Who Noticed:** _____

**Who Left The Room:** _____

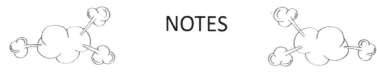

# NOTES

_____
_____
_____
_____
_____
_____
_____
_____
_____
_____
_____

# NOTES

_____
_____
_____
_____
_____
_____
_____
_____
_____
_____

**Date:** ___ / ___ / ___     Sun  Mon  Tue  Wed  Thu  Fri  Sat

**Time of Fart:** _____ am/pm     **Duration:** ___ min ___ sec

**Fart Intensity:**
- ○ **Gentle Puff** (barely there, quick & unscented)
- ○ **SBD** (silent but deadly)
- ○ **Military March** (series of puffs with mild scent)
- ○ **Classic** (quick, loud, stinky scent but fades quickly)
- ○ **Thunder Rumble** (long, loud & stinky)
- ○ **Diarrhea Storm** (explosive, wet & clears the room)
- ○ **Oh, Crap!** (self explanatory)

**Fart Enjoyment Scale:**  ☺  ☺  ☺  ☺  ☺

**Who Noticed:** _____

**Who Left The Room:** _____

---

**Date:** ___ / ___ / ___     Sun  Mon  Tue  Wed  Thu  Fri  Sat

**Time of Fart:** _____ am/pm     **Duration:** ___ min ___ sec

**Fart Intensity:**
- ○ **Gentle Puff** (barely there, quick & unscented)
- ○ **SBD** (silent but deadly)
- ○ **Military March** (series of puffs with mild scent)
- ○ **Classic** (quick, loud, stinky scent but fades quickly)
- ○ **Thunder Rumble** (long, loud & stinky)
- ○ **Diarrhea Storm** (explosive, wet & clears the room)
- ○ **Oh, Crap!** (self explanatory)

**Fart Enjoyment Scale:**  ☺  ☺  ☺  ☺  ☺

**Who Noticed:** _____

**Who Left The Room:** _____

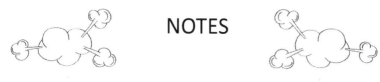

# NOTES

_____
_____
_____
_____
_____
_____
_____
_____
_____
_____
_____
_____

# NOTES

_____
_____
_____
_____
_____
_____
_____
_____
_____
_____

**Date:** ___ / ___ / ___     Sun   Mon   Tue   Wed   Thu   Fri   Sat

**Time of Fart:** _____ am/pm     **Duration:** ___ min ___ sec

**Fart Intensity:**
- ○ **Gentle Puff** (barely there, quick & unscented)
- ○ **SBD** (silent but deadly)
- ○ **Military March** (series of puffs with mild scent)
- ○ **Classic** (quick, loud, stinky scent but fades quickly)
- ○ **Thunder Rumble** (long, loud & stinky)
- ○ **Diarrhea Storm** (explosive, wet & clears the room)
- ○ **Oh, Crap!** (self explanatory)

**Fart Enjoyment Scale:**  ☺ ☺ ☺ ☺ ☺

**Who Noticed:** _____

**Who Left The Room:** _____

---

**Date:** ___ / ___ / ___     Sun   Mon   Tue   Wed   Thu   Fri   Sat

**Time of Fart:** _____ am/pm     **Duration:** ___ min ___ sec

**Fart Intensity:**
- ○ **Gentle Puff** (barely there, quick & unscented)
- ○ **SBD** (silent but deadly)
- ○ **Military March** (series of puffs with mild scent)
- ○ **Classic** (quick, loud, stinky scent but fades quickly)
- ○ **Thunder Rumble** (long, loud & stinky)
- ○ **Diarrhea Storm** (explosive, wet & clears the room)
- ○ **Oh, Crap!** (self explanatory)

**Fart Enjoyment Scale:**  ☺ ☺ ☺ ☺ ☺

**Who Noticed:** _____

**Who Left The Room:** _____

# NOTES

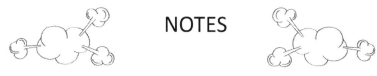

_____

_____

_____

_____

_____

_____

_____

_____

_____

_____

# NOTES

_____

_____

_____

_____

_____

_____

_____

_____

_____

**Date:** ___ / ___ / ___    Sun  Mon  Tue  Wed  Thu  Fri  Sat

**Time of Fart:** _____ am/pm    **Duration:** ___ min ___ sec

**Fart Intensity:**
- ○ **Gentle Puff** (barely there, quick & unscented)
- ○ **SBD** (silent but deadly)
- ○ **Military March** (series of puffs with mild scent)
- ○ **Classic** (quick, loud, stinky scent but fades quickly)
- ○ **Thunder Rumble** (long, loud & stinky)
- ○ **Diarrhea Storm** (explosive, wet & clears the room)
- ○ **Oh, Crap!** (self explanatory)

**Fart Enjoyment Scale:** ☺ ☺ ☺ ☺ ☺

**Who Noticed:** _____

**Who Left The Room:** _____

---

**Date:** ___ / ___ / ___    Sun  Mon  Tue  Wed  Thu  Fri  Sat

**Time of Fart:** _____ am/pm    **Duration:** ___ min ___ sec

**Fart Intensity:**
- ○ **Gentle Puff** (barely there, quick & unscented)
- ○ **SBD** (silent but deadly)
- ○ **Military March** (series of puffs with mild scent)
- ○ **Classic** (quick, loud, stinky scent but fades quickly)
- ○ **Thunder Rumble** (long, loud & stinky)
- ○ **Diarrhea Storm** (explosive, wet & clears the room)
- ○ **Oh, Crap!** (self explanatory)

**Fart Enjoyment Scale:** ☺ ☺ ☺ ☺ ☺

**Who Noticed:** _____

**Who Left The Room:** _____

# NOTES

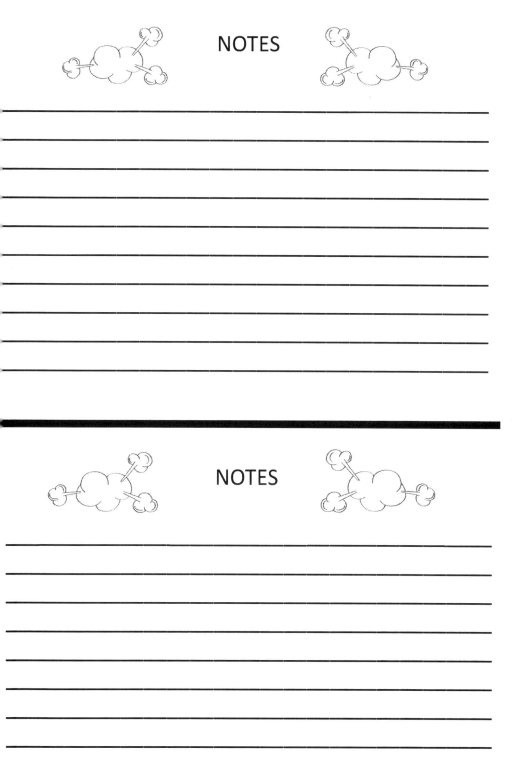

# NOTES

**Date:** ___ / ___ / ___     Sun  Mon  Tue  Wed  Thu  Fri  Sat

**Time of Fart:** _____ am/pm     **Duration:** ____ min ____ sec

**Fart Intensity:**
- ○ **Gentle Puff** (barely there, quick & unscented)
- ○ **SBD** (silent but deadly)
- ○ **Military March** (series of puffs with mild scent)
- ○ **Classic** (quick, loud, stinky scent but fades quickly)
- ○ **Thunder Rumble** (long, loud & stinky)
- ○ **Diarrhea Storm** (explosive, wet & clears the room)
- ○ **Oh, Crap!** (self explanatory)

**Fart Enjoyment Scale:**  ☺ ☺ ☺ ☺ ☺

**Who Noticed:** _____

**Who Left The Room:** _____

---

**Date:** ___ / ___ / ___     Sun  Mon  Tue  Wed  Thu  Fri  Sat

**Time of Fart:** _____ am/pm     **Duration:** ____ min ____ sec

**Fart Intensity:**
- ○ **Gentle Puff** (barely there, quick & unscented)
- ○ **SBD** (silent but deadly)
- ○ **Military March** (series of puffs with mild scent)
- ○ **Classic** (quick, loud, stinky scent but fades quickly)
- ○ **Thunder Rumble** (long, loud & stinky)
- ○ **Diarrhea Storm** (explosive, wet & clears the room)
- ○ **Oh, Crap!** (self explanatory)

**Fart Enjoyment Scale:**  ☺ ☺ ☺ ☺ ☺

**Who Noticed:** _____

**Who Left The Room:** _____

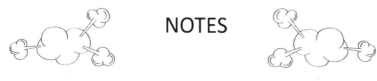

# NOTES

_____
_____
_____
_____
_____
_____
_____
_____
_____
_____
_____

# NOTES

_____
_____
_____
_____
_____
_____
_____
_____
_____

**Date:** ___ / ___ / ___     Sun  Mon  Tue  Wed  Thu  Fri  Sat

**Time of Fart:** _____ am/pm     **Duration:** ___ min ___ sec

**Fart Intensity:**
- ○ **Gentle Puff** (barely there, quick & unscented)
- ○ **SBD** (silent but deadly)
- ○ **Military March** (series of puffs with mild scent)
- ○ **Classic** (quick, loud, stinky scent but fades quickly)
- ○ **Thunder Rumble** (long, loud & stinky)
- ○ **Diarrhea Storm** (explosive, wet & clears the room)
- ○ **Oh, Crap!** (self explanatory)

**Fart Enjoyment Scale:**  ☺ ☺ ☺ ☺ ☺

**Who Noticed:** _____

**Who Left The Room:** _____

---

**Date:** ___ / ___ / ___     Sun  Mon  Tue  Wed  Thu  Fri  Sat

**Time of Fart:** _____ am/pm     **Duration:** ___ min ___ sec

**Fart Intensity:**
- ○ **Gentle Puff** (barely there, quick & unscented)
- ○ **SBD** (silent but deadly)
- ○ **Military March** (series of puffs with mild scent)
- ○ **Classic** (quick, loud, stinky scent but fades quickly)
- ○ **Thunder Rumble** (long, loud & stinky)
- ○ **Diarrhea Storm** (explosive, wet & clears the room)
- ○ **Oh, Crap!** (self explanatory)

**Fart Enjoyment Scale:**  ☺ ☺ ☺ ☺ ☺

**Who Noticed:** _____

**Who Left The Room:** _____

# NOTES

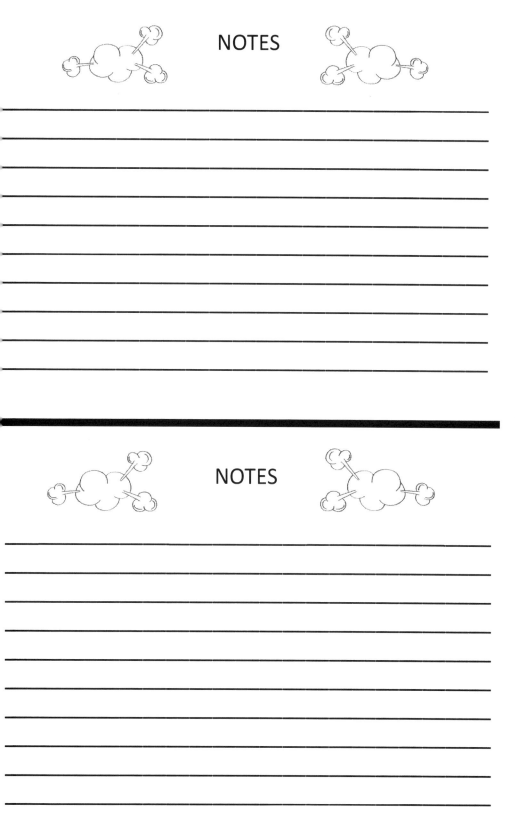

# NOTES

**Date:** ___ / ___ / ___     Sun  Mon  Tue  Wed  Thu  Fri  Sat

**Time of Fart:** _____ am/pm     **Duration:** ___ min ___ sec

**Fart Intensity:**
- ○ **Gentle Puff** (barely there, quick & unscented)
- ○ **SBD** (silent but deadly)
- ○ **Military March** (series of puffs with mild scent)
- ○ **Classic** (quick, loud, stinky scent but fades quickly)
- ○ **Thunder Rumble** (long, loud & stinky)
- ○ **Diarrhea Storm** (explosive, wet & clears the room)
- ○ **Oh, Crap!** (self explanatory)

**Fart Enjoyment Scale:** ☺ ☺ ☺ ☺ ☺

**Who Noticed:** _____

**Who Left The Room:** _____

---

**Date:** ___ / ___ / ___     Sun  Mon  Tue  Wed  Thu  Fri  Sat

**Time of Fart:** _____ am/pm     **Duration:** ___ min ___ sec

**Fart Intensity:**
- ○ **Gentle Puff** (barely there, quick & unscented)
- ○ **SBD** (silent but deadly)
- ○ **Military March** (series of puffs with mild scent)
- ○ **Classic** (quick, loud, stinky scent but fades quickly)
- ○ **Thunder Rumble** (long, loud & stinky)
- ○ **Diarrhea Storm** (explosive, wet & clears the room)
- ○ **Oh, Crap!** (self explanatory)

**Fart Enjoyment Scale:** ☺ ☺ ☺ ☺ ☺

**Who Noticed:** _____

**Who Left The Room:** _____

# NOTES

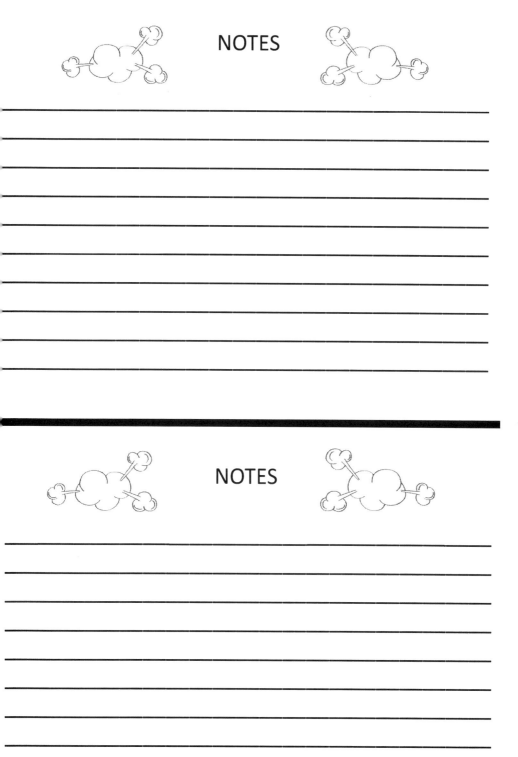

# NOTES

**Date:** ___ / ___ / ___     Sun  Mon  Tue  Wed  Thu  Fri  Sat

**Time of Fart:** _____ am/pm     **Duration:** ____ min ____ sec

**Fart Intensity:**
- ○ **Gentle Puff** (barely there, quick & unscented)
- ○ **SBD** (silent but deadly)
- ○ **Military March** (series of puffs with mild scent)
- ○ **Classic** (quick, loud, stinky scent but fades quickly)
- ○ **Thunder Rumble** (long, loud & stinky)
- ○ **Diarrhea Storm** (explosive, wet & clears the room)
- ○ **Oh, Crap!** (self explanatory)

**Fart Enjoyment Scale:** ☺ ☺ ☺ ☺ ☺

**Who Noticed:** _____

**Who Left The Room:** _____

---

**Date:** ___ / ___ / ___     Sun  Mon  Tue  Wed  Thu  Fri  Sat

**Time of Fart:** _____ am/pm     **Duration:** ____ min ____ sec

**Fart Intensity:**
- ○ **Gentle Puff** (barely there, quick & unscented)
- ○ **SBD** (silent but deadly)
- ○ **Military March** (series of puffs with mild scent)
- ○ **Classic** (quick, loud, stinky scent but fades quickly)
- ○ **Thunder Rumble** (long, loud & stinky)
- ○ **Diarrhea Storm** (explosive, wet & clears the room)
- ○ **Oh, Crap!** (self explanatory)

**Fart Enjoyment Scale:** ☺ ☺ ☺ ☺ ☺

**Who Noticed:** _____

**Who Left The Room:** _____

# NOTES

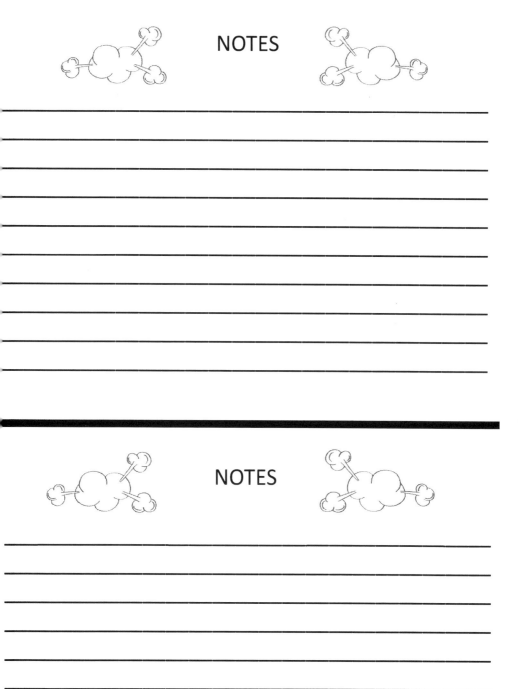

# NOTES

**Date:** ___ / ___ / ___     Sun  Mon  Tue  Wed  Thu  Fri  Sat

**Time of Fart:** _____ am/pm     **Duration:** ___ min ___ sec

**Fart Intensity:**
- ○  **Gentle Puff** (barely there, quick & unscented)
- ○  **SBD** (silent but deadly)
- ○  **Military March** (series of puffs with mild scent)
- ○  **Classic** (quick, loud, stinky scent but fades quickly)
- ○  **Thunder Rumble** (long, loud & stinky)
- ○  **Diarrhea Storm** (explosive, wet & clears the room)
- ○  **Oh, Crap!** (self explanatory)

**Fart Enjoyment Scale:**  ☺ ☺ ☺ ☺ ☺

**Who Noticed:** _____

**Who Left The Room:** _____

---

**Date:** ___ / ___ / ___     Sun  Mon  Tue  Wed  Thu  Fri  Sat

**Time of Fart:** _____ am/pm     **Duration:** ___ min ___ sec

**Fart Intensity:**
- ○  **Gentle Puff** (barely there, quick & unscented)
- ○  **SBD** (silent but deadly)
- ○  **Military March** (series of puffs with mild scent)
- ○  **Classic** (quick, loud, stinky scent but fades quickly)
- ○  **Thunder Rumble** (long, loud & stinky)
- ○  **Diarrhea Storm** (explosive, wet & clears the room)
- ○  **Oh, Crap!** (self explanatory)

**Fart Enjoyment Scale:**  ☺ ☺ ☺ ☺ ☺

**Who Noticed:** _____

**Who Left The Room:** _____

# NOTES

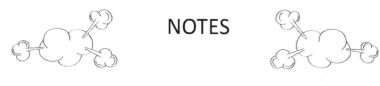

_____
_____
_____
_____
_____
_____
_____
_____
_____
_____

# NOTES

_____
_____
_____
_____
_____
_____
_____
_____
_____

**Date:** ___ / ___ / ___    Sun  Mon  Tue  Wed  Thu  Fri  Sat

**Time of Fart:** _____ am/pm    **Duration:** ____ min ____ sec

**Fart Intensity:**
- ○ **Gentle Puff** (barely there, quick & unscented)
- ○ **SBD** (silent but deadly)
- ○ **Military March** (series of puffs with mild scent)
- ○ **Classic** (quick, loud, stinky scent but fades quickly)
- ○ **Thunder Rumble** (long, loud & stinky)
- ○ **Diarrhea Storm** (explosive, wet & clears the room)
- ○ **Oh, Crap!** (self explanatory)

**Fart Enjoyment Scale:** ☺ ☺ ☺ ☺ ☺

**Who Noticed:** _____

**Who Left The Room:** _____

---

**Date:** ___ / ___ / ___    Sun  Mon  Tue  Wed  Thu  Fri  Sat

**Time of Fart:** _____ am/pm    **Duration:** ____ min ____ sec

**Fart Intensity:**
- ○ **Gentle Puff** (barely there, quick & unscented)
- ○ **SBD** (silent but deadly)
- ○ **Military March** (series of puffs with mild scent)
- ○ **Classic** (quick, loud, stinky scent but fades quickly)
- ○ **Thunder Rumble** (long, loud & stinky)
- ○ **Diarrhea Storm** (explosive, wet & clears the room)
- ○ **Oh, Crap!** (self explanatory)

**Fart Enjoyment Scale:** ☺ ☺ ☺ ☺ ☺

**Who Noticed:** _____

**Who Left The Room:** _____

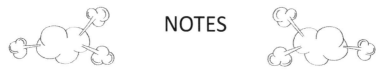

# NOTES

_____

_____

_____

_____

_____

_____

_____

_____

_____

_____

_____

# NOTES

_____

_____

_____

_____

_____

_____

_____

_____

_____

**Date:** ___ / ___ / ___    Sun  Mon  Tue  Wed  Thu  Fri  Sat

**Time of Fart:** _____ am/pm    **Duration:** ___ min ___ sec

**Fart Intensity:**
- ○  **Gentle Puff** (barely there, quick & unscented)
- ○  **SBD** (silent but deadly)
- ○  **Military March** (series of puffs with mild scent)
- ○  **Classic** (quick, loud, stinky scent but fades quickly)
- ○  **Thunder Rumble** (long, loud & stinky)
- ○  **Diarrhea Storm** (explosive, wet & clears the room)
- ○  **Oh, Crap!** (self explanatory)

**Fart Enjoyment Scale:**  ☺ ☺ ☺ ☺ ☺

**Who Noticed:** _____

**Who Left The Room:** _____

---

**Date:** ___ / ___ / ___    Sun  Mon  Tue  Wed  Thu  Fri  Sat

**Time of Fart:** _____ am/pm    **Duration:** ___ min ___ sec

**Fart Intensity:**
- ○  **Gentle Puff** (barely there, quick & unscented)
- ○  **SBD** (silent but deadly)
- ○  **Military March** (series of puffs with mild scent)
- ○  **Classic** (quick, loud, stinky scent but fades quickly)
- ○  **Thunder Rumble** (long, loud & stinky)
- ○  **Diarrhea Storm** (explosive, wet & clears the room)
- ○  **Oh, Crap!** (self explanatory)

**Fart Enjoyment Scale:**  ☺ ☺ ☺ ☺ ☺

**Who Noticed:** _____

**Who Left The Room:** _____

# NOTES

# NOTES

**Date:** ___ / ___ / ___     Sun  Mon  Tue  Wed  Thu  Fri  Sat

**Time of Fart:** _____ am/pm     **Duration:** ___ min ___ sec

**Fart Intensity:**
- ○ **Gentle Puff** (barely there, quick & unscented)
- ○ **SBD** (silent but deadly)
- ○ **Military March** (series of puffs with mild scent)
- ○ **Classic** (quick, loud, stinky scent but fades quickly)
- ○ **Thunder Rumble** (long, loud & stinky)
- ○ **Diarrhea Storm** (explosive, wet & clears the room)
- ○ **Oh, Crap!** (self explanatory)

**Fart Enjoyment Scale:** ☺ ☺ ☺ ☺ ☺

**Who Noticed:** _____

**Who Left The Room:** _____

---

**Date:** ___ / ___ / ___     Sun  Mon  Tue  Wed  Thu  Fri  Sat

**Time of Fart:** _____ am/pm     **Duration:** ___ min ___ sec

**Fart Intensity:**
- ○ **Gentle Puff** (barely there, quick & unscented)
- ○ **SBD** (silent but deadly)
- ○ **Military March** (series of puffs with mild scent)
- ○ **Classic** (quick, loud, stinky scent but fades quickly)
- ○ **Thunder Rumble** (long, loud & stinky)
- ○ **Diarrhea Storm** (explosive, wet & clears the room)
- ○ **Oh, Crap!** (self explanatory)

**Fart Enjoyment Scale:** ☺ ☺ ☺ ☺ ☺

**Who Noticed:** _____

**Who Left The Room:** _____

# NOTES

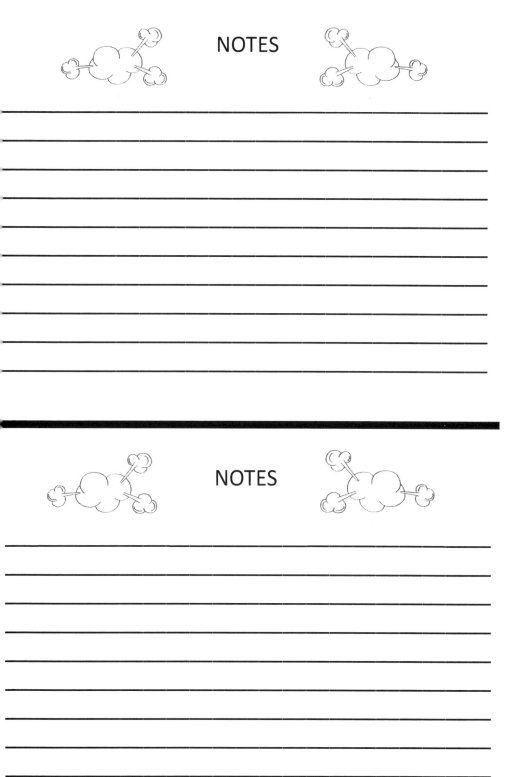

# NOTES

**Date:** ___ / ___ / ___    Sun   Mon   Tue   Wed   Thu   Fri   Sat

**Time of Fart:** _____ am/pm    **Duration:** ____ min ____ sec

**Fart Intensity:**
- ○ **Gentle Puff** (barely there, quick & unscented)
- ○ **SBD** (silent but deadly)
- ○ **Military March** (series of puffs with mild scent)
- ○ **Classic** (quick, loud, stinky scent but fades quickly)
- ○ **Thunder Rumble** (long, loud & stinky)
- ○ **Diarrhea Storm** (explosive, wet & clears the room)
- ○ **Oh, Crap!** (self explanatory)

**Fart Enjoyment Scale:** ☺ ☺ ☺ ☺ ☺

**Who Noticed:** _____

**Who Left The Room:** _____

---

**Date:** ___ / ___ / ___    Sun   Mon   Tue   Wed   Thu   Fri   Sat

**Time of Fart:** _____ am/pm    **Duration:** ____ min ____ sec

**Fart Intensity:**
- ○ **Gentle Puff** (barely there, quick & unscented)
- ○ **SBD** (silent but deadly)
- ○ **Military March** (series of puffs with mild scent)
- ○ **Classic** (quick, loud, stinky scent but fades quickly)
- ○ **Thunder Rumble** (long, loud & stinky)
- ○ **Diarrhea Storm** (explosive, wet & clears the room)
- ○ **Oh, Crap!** (self explanatory)

**Fart Enjoyment Scale:** ☺ ☺ ☺ ☺ ☺

**Who Noticed:** _____

**Who Left The Room:** _____

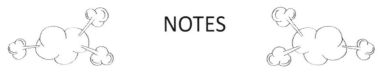

# NOTES

_____
_____
_____
_____
_____
_____
_____
_____
_____
_____
_____
_____

# NOTES

_____
_____
_____
_____
_____
_____
_____
_____
_____
_____
_____

**Date:** ___ / ___ / ___     Sun  Mon  Tue  Wed  Thu  Fri  Sat

**Time of Fart:** _____ am/pm     **Duration:** ___ min ___ sec

**Fart Intensity:**
- ○ **Gentle Puff** (barely there, quick & unscented)
- ○ **SBD** (silent but deadly)
- ○ **Military March** (series of puffs with mild scent)
- ○ **Classic** (quick, loud, stinky scent but fades quickly)
- ○ **Thunder Rumble** (long, loud & stinky)
- ○ **Diarrhea Storm** (explosive, wet & clears the room)
- ○ **Oh, Crap!** (self explanatory)

**Fart Enjoyment Scale:**  ☺ ☺ ☺ ☺ ☺

**Who Noticed:** _____

**Who Left The Room:** _____

---

**Date:** ___ / ___ / ___     Sun  Mon  Tue  Wed  Thu  Fri  Sat

**Time of Fart:** _____ am/pm     **Duration:** ___ min ___ sec

**Fart Intensity:**
- ○ **Gentle Puff** (barely there, quick & unscented)
- ○ **SBD** (silent but deadly)
- ○ **Military March** (series of puffs with mild scent)
- ○ **Classic** (quick, loud, stinky scent but fades quickly)
- ○ **Thunder Rumble** (long, loud & stinky)
- ○ **Diarrhea Storm** (explosive, wet & clears the room)
- ○ **Oh, Crap!** (self explanatory)

**Fart Enjoyment Scale:**  ☺ ☺ ☺ ☺ ☺

**Who Noticed:** _____

**Who Left The Room:** _____

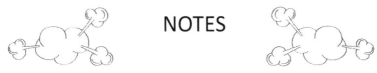

# NOTES

_____

_____

_____

_____

_____

_____

_____

_____

_____

_____

_____

_____

# NOTES

_____

_____

_____

_____

_____

_____

_____

_____

_____

_____

**Date:** ___ / ___ / ___     Sun  Mon  Tue  Wed  Thu  Fri  Sat

**Time of Fart:** _____ am/pm     **Duration:** ___ min ___ sec

**Fart Intensity:**
- ○ **Gentle Puff** (barely there, quick & unscented)
- ○ **SBD** (silent but deadly)
- ○ **Military March** (series of puffs with mild scent)
- ○ **Classic** (quick, loud, stinky scent but fades quickly)
- ○ **Thunder Rumble** (long, loud & stinky)
- ○ **Diarrhea Storm** (explosive, wet & clears the room)
- ○ **Oh, Crap!** (self explanatory)

**Fart Enjoyment Scale:**  ☺ ☺ ☺ ☺ ☺

**Who Noticed:** _____

**Who Left The Room:** _____

---

**Date:** ___ / ___ / ___     Sun  Mon  Tue  Wed  Thu  Fri  Sat

**Time of Fart:** _____ am/pm     **Duration:** ___ min ___ sec

**Fart Intensity:**
- ○ **Gentle Puff** (barely there, quick & unscented)
- ○ **SBD** (silent but deadly)
- ○ **Military March** (series of puffs with mild scent)
- ○ **Classic** (quick, loud, stinky scent but fades quickly)
- ○ **Thunder Rumble** (long, loud & stinky)
- ○ **Diarrhea Storm** (explosive, wet & clears the room)
- ○ **Oh, Crap!** (self explanatory)

**Fart Enjoyment Scale:**  ☺ ☺ ☺ ☺ ☺

**Who Noticed:** _____

**Who Left The Room:** _____

# NOTES

_____

_____

_____

_____

_____

_____

_____

_____

_____

_____

_____

_____

# NOTES

_____

_____

_____

_____

_____

_____

_____

_____

_____

**Date:** ___ / ___ / ___     Sun  Mon  Tue  Wed  Thu  Fri  Sat

**Time of Fart:** _____ am/pm     **Duration:** ___ min ___ sec

**Fart Intensity:**
- ○ **Gentle Puff** (barely there, quick & unscented)
- ○ **SBD** (silent but deadly)
- ○ **Military March** (series of puffs with mild scent)
- ○ **Classic** (quick, loud, stinky scent but fades quickly)
- ○ **Thunder Rumble** (long, loud & stinky)
- ○ **Diarrhea Storm** (explosive, wet & clears the room)
- ○ **Oh, Crap!** (self explanatory)

**Fart Enjoyment Scale:**  ☺ ☺ ☺ ☺ ☺

**Who Noticed:** _____

**Who Left The Room:** _____

---

**Date:** ___ / ___ / ___     Sun  Mon  Tue  Wed  Thu  Fri  Sat

**Time of Fart:** _____ am/pm     **Duration:** ___ min ___ sec

**Fart Intensity:**
- ○ **Gentle Puff** (barely there, quick & unscented)
- ○ **SBD** (silent but deadly)
- ○ **Military March** (series of puffs with mild scent)
- ○ **Classic** (quick, loud, stinky scent but fades quickly)
- ○ **Thunder Rumble** (long, loud & stinky)
- ○ **Diarrhea Storm** (explosive, wet & clears the room)
- ○ **Oh, Crap!** (self explanatory)

**Fart Enjoyment Scale:**  ☺ ☺ ☺ ☺ ☺

**Who Noticed:** _____

**Who Left The Room:** _____

# NOTES

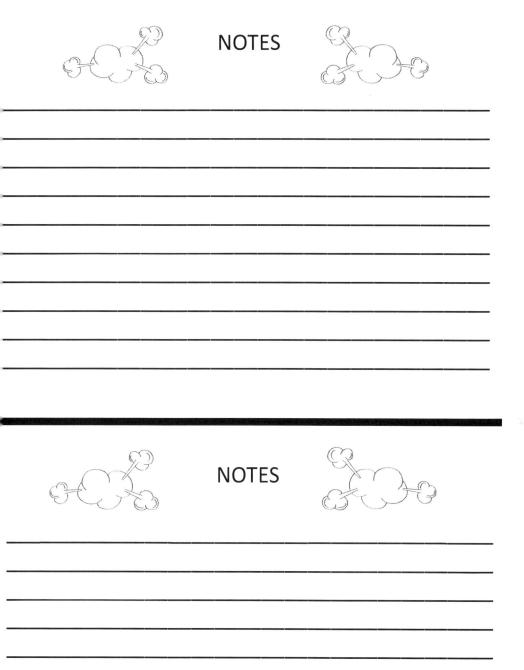

# NOTES

**Date:** ___ / ___ / ___     Sun  Mon  Tue  Wed  Thu  Fri  Sat

**Time of Fart:** _____ am/pm     **Duration:** ___ min ___ sec

**Fart Intensity:**
- ○ **Gentle Puff** (barely there, quick & unscented)
- ○ **SBD** (silent but deadly)
- ○ **Military March** (series of puffs with mild scent)
- ○ **Classic** (quick, loud, stinky scent but fades quickly)
- ○ **Thunder Rumble** (long, loud & stinky)
- ○ **Diarrhea Storm** (explosive, wet & clears the room)
- ○ **Oh, Crap!** (self explanatory)

**Fart Enjoyment Scale:**  ☺ ☺ ☺ ☺ ☺

**Who Noticed:** _____

**Who Left The Room:** _____

---

**Date:** ___ / ___ / ___     Sun  Mon  Tue  Wed  Thu  Fri  Sat

**Time of Fart:** _____ am/pm     **Duration:** ___ min ___ sec

**Fart Intensity:**
- ○ **Gentle Puff** (barely there, quick & unscented)
- ○ **SBD** (silent but deadly)
- ○ **Military March** (series of puffs with mild scent)
- ○ **Classic** (quick, loud, stinky scent but fades quickly)
- ○ **Thunder Rumble** (long, loud & stinky)
- ○ **Diarrhea Storm** (explosive, wet & clears the room)
- ○ **Oh, Crap!** (self explanatory)

**Fart Enjoyment Scale:**  ☺ ☺ ☺ ☺ ☺

**Who Noticed:** _____

**Who Left The Room:** _____

# NOTES

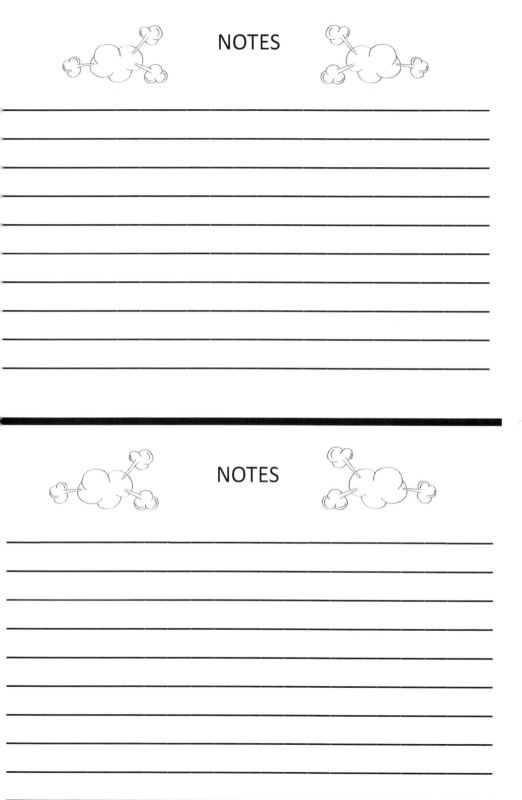

# NOTES

**Date:** ___ / ___ / ___    Sun  Mon  Tue  Wed  Thu  Fri  Sat

**Time of Fart:** _____ am/pm    **Duration:** ___ min ___ sec

**Fart Intensity:**
- ○ **Gentle Puff** (barely there, quick & unscented)
- ○ **SBD** (silent but deadly)
- ○ **Military March** (series of puffs with mild scent)
- ○ **Classic** (quick, loud, stinky scent but fades quickly)
- ○ **Thunder Rumble** (long, loud & stinky)
- ○ **Diarrhea Storm** (explosive, wet & clears the room)
- ○ **Oh, Crap!** (self explanatory)

**Fart Enjoyment Scale:**  ☺  ☺  ☺  ☺  ☺

**Who Noticed:** _____

**Who Left The Room:** _____

---

**Date:** ___ / ___ / ___    Sun  Mon  Tue  Wed  Thu  Fri  Sat

**Time of Fart:** _____ am/pm    **Duration:** ___ min ___ sec

**Fart Intensity:**
- ○ **Gentle Puff** (barely there, quick & unscented)
- ○ **SBD** (silent but deadly)
- ○ **Military March** (series of puffs with mild scent)
- ○ **Classic** (quick, loud, stinky scent but fades quickly)
- ○ **Thunder Rumble** (long, loud & stinky)
- ○ **Diarrhea Storm** (explosive, wet & clears the room)
- ○ **Oh, Crap!** (self explanatory)

**Fart Enjoyment Scale:**  ☺  ☺  ☺  ☺  ☺

**Who Noticed:** _____

**Who Left The Room:** _____

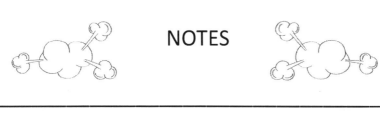

# NOTES

_____

_____

_____

_____

_____

_____

_____

_____

_____

_____

_____

# NOTES

_____

_____

_____

_____

_____

_____

_____

_____

_____

**Date:** ___ / ___ / ___     Sun   Mon   Tue   Wed   Thu   Fri   Sat

**Time of Fart:** _____ am/pm     **Duration:** ____ min ____ sec

**Fart Intensity:**
- ○ **Gentle Puff** (barely there, quick & unscented)
- ○ **SBD** (silent but deadly)
- ○ **Military March** (series of puffs with mild scent)
- ○ **Classic** (quick, loud, stinky scent but fades quickly)
- ○ **Thunder Rumble** (long, loud & stinky)
- ○ **Diarrhea Storm** (explosive, wet & clears the room)
- ○ **Oh, Crap!** (self explanatory)

**Fart Enjoyment Scale:**  ☺ ☺ ☺ ☺ ☺

**Who Noticed:** _____

**Who Left The Room:** _____

---

**Date:** ___ / ___ / ___     Sun   Mon   Tue   Wed   Thu   Fri   Sat

**Time of Fart:** _____ am/pm     **Duration:** ____ min ____ sec

**Fart Intensity:**
- ○ **Gentle Puff** (barely there, quick & unscented)
- ○ **SBD** (silent but deadly)
- ○ **Military March** (series of puffs with mild scent)
- ○ **Classic** (quick, loud, stinky scent but fades quickly)
- ○ **Thunder Rumble** (long, loud & stinky)
- ○ **Diarrhea Storm** (explosive, wet & clears the room)
- ○ **Oh, Crap!** (self explanatory)

**Fart Enjoyment Scale:**  ☺ ☺ ☺ ☺ ☺

**Who Noticed:** _____

**Who Left The Room:** _____

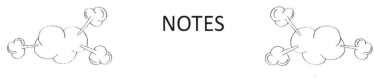

# NOTES

_____
_____
_____
_____
_____
_____
_____
_____
_____
_____
_____

# NOTES

_____
_____
_____
_____
_____
_____
_____
_____
_____

**Date:** \_\_\_ / \_\_\_ / \_\_\_    Sun  Mon  Tue  Wed  Thu  Fri  Sat

**Time of Fart:** _____ am/pm    **Duration:** \_\_\_\_ min \_\_\_\_ sec

**Fart Intensity:**
- ○ **Gentle Puff** (barely there, quick & unscented)
- ○ **SBD** (silent but deadly)
- ○ **Military March** (series of puffs with mild scent)
- ○ **Classic** (quick, loud, stinky scent but fades quickly)
- ○ **Thunder Rumble** (long, loud & stinky)
- ○ **Diarrhea Storm** (explosive, wet & clears the room)
- ○ **Oh, Crap!** (self explanatory)

**Fart Enjoyment Scale:**  ☺ ☺ ☺ ☺ ☺

**Who Noticed:** _____

**Who Left The Room:** _____

---

**Date:** \_\_\_ / \_\_\_ / \_\_\_    Sun  Mon  Tue  Wed  Thu  Fri  Sat

**Time of Fart:** _____ am/pm    **Duration:** \_\_\_\_ min \_\_\_\_ sec

**Fart Intensity:**
- ○ **Gentle Puff** (barely there, quick & unscented)
- ○ **SBD** (silent but deadly)
- ○ **Military March** (series of puffs with mild scent)
- ○ **Classic** (quick, loud, stinky scent but fades quickly)
- ○ **Thunder Rumble** (long, loud & stinky)
- ○ **Diarrhea Storm** (explosive, wet & clears the room)
- ○ **Oh, Crap!** (self explanatory)

**Fart Enjoyment Scale:**  ☺ ☺ ☺ ☺ ☺

**Who Noticed:** _____

**Who Left The Room:** _____

# NOTES

---

---

---

---

---

---

---

---

---

---

---

---

# NOTES

---

---

---

---

---

---

---

---

---

---

---

**Date:** ___ / ___ / ___  Sun  Mon  Tue  Wed  Thu  Fri  Sat

**Time of Fart:** _____ am/pm  **Duration:** ___ min ___ sec

**Fart Intensity:**
- ○ **Gentle Puff** (barely there, quick & unscented)
- ○ **SBD** (silent but deadly)
- ○ **Military March** (series of puffs with mild scent)
- ○ **Classic** (quick, loud, stinky scent but fades quickly)
- ○ **Thunder Rumble** (long, loud & stinky)
- ○ **Diarrhea Storm** (explosive, wet & clears the room)
- ○ **Oh, Crap!** (self explanatory)

**Fart Enjoyment Scale:** ☺ ☺ ☺ ☺ ☺

**Who Noticed:** _____

**Who Left The Room:** _____

---

**Date:** ___ / ___ / ___  Sun  Mon  Tue  Wed  Thu  Fri  Sat

**Time of Fart:** _____ am/pm  **Duration:** ___ min ___ sec

**Fart Intensity:**
- ○ **Gentle Puff** (barely there, quick & unscented)
- ○ **SBD** (silent but deadly)
- ○ **Military March** (series of puffs with mild scent)
- ○ **Classic** (quick, loud, stinky scent but fades quickly)
- ○ **Thunder Rumble** (long, loud & stinky)
- ○ **Diarrhea Storm** (explosive, wet & clears the room)
- ○ **Oh, Crap!** (self explanatory)

**Fart Enjoyment Scale:** ☺ ☺ ☺ ☺ ☺

**Who Noticed:** _____

**Who Left The Room:** _____

# NOTES

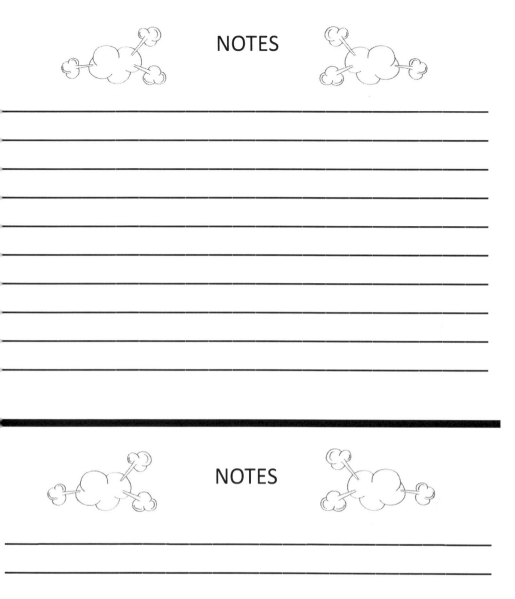

# NOTES

**Date:** ___ / ___ / ___    Sun  Mon  Tue  Wed  Thu  Fri  Sat

**Time of Fart:** _____ am/pm    **Duration:** ___ min ___ sec

**Fart Intensity:**
- ○ **Gentle Puff** (barely there, quick & unscented)
- ○ **SBD** (silent but deadly)
- ○ **Military March** (series of puffs with mild scent)
- ○ **Classic** (quick, loud, stinky scent but fades quickly)
- ○ **Thunder Rumble** (long, loud & stinky)
- ○ **Diarrhea Storm** (explosive, wet & clears the room)
- ○ **Oh, Crap!** (self explanatory)

**Fart Enjoyment Scale:**  ☺ ☺ ☺ ☺ ☺

**Who Noticed:** _____

**Who Left The Room:** _____

---

**Date:** ___ / ___ / ___    Sun  Mon  Tue  Wed  Thu  Fri  Sat

**Time of Fart:** _____ am/pm    **Duration:** ___ min ___ sec

**Fart Intensity:**
- ○ **Gentle Puff** (barely there, quick & unscented)
- ○ **SBD** (silent but deadly)
- ○ **Military March** (series of puffs with mild scent)
- ○ **Classic** (quick, loud, stinky scent but fades quickly)
- ○ **Thunder Rumble** (long, loud & stinky)
- ○ **Diarrhea Storm** (explosive, wet & clears the room)
- ○ **Oh, Crap!** (self explanatory)

**Fart Enjoyment Scale:**  ☺ ☺ ☺ ☺ ☺

**Who Noticed:** _____

**Who Left The Room:** _____

# NOTES

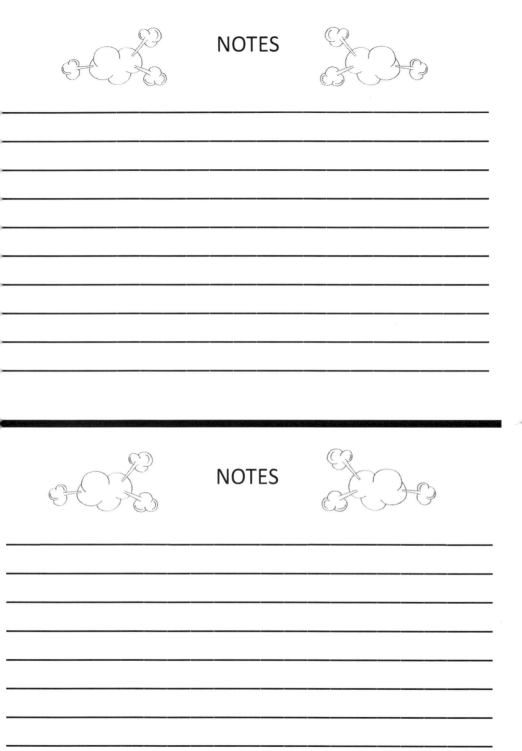

# NOTES

**Date:** ___ / ___ / ___     Sun  Mon  Tue  Wed  Thu  Fri  Sat

**Time of Fart:** _____ am/pm     **Duration:** ___ min ___ sec

**Fart Intensity:**
- ○ **Gentle Puff** (barely there, quick & unscented)
- ○ **SBD** (silent but deadly)
- ○ **Military March** (series of puffs with mild scent)
- ○ **Classic** (quick, loud, stinky scent but fades quickly)
- ○ **Thunder Rumble** (long, loud & stinky)
- ○ **Diarrhea Storm** (explosive, wet & clears the room)
- ○ **Oh, Crap!** (self explanatory)

**Fart Enjoyment Scale:**  ☺ ☺ ☺ ☺ ☺

**Who Noticed:** _____

**Who Left The Room:** _____

---

**Date:** ___ / ___ / ___     Sun  Mon  Tue  Wed  Thu  Fri  Sat

**Time of Fart:** _____ am/pm     **Duration:** ___ min ___ sec

**Fart Intensity:**
- ○ **Gentle Puff** (barely there, quick & unscented)
- ○ **SBD** (silent but deadly)
- ○ **Military March** (series of puffs with mild scent)
- ○ **Classic** (quick, loud, stinky scent but fades quickly)
- ○ **Thunder Rumble** (long, loud & stinky)
- ○ **Diarrhea Storm** (explosive, wet & clears the room)
- ○ **Oh, Crap!** (self explanatory)

**Fart Enjoyment Scale:**  ☺ ☺ ☺ ☺ ☺

**Who Noticed:** _____

**Who Left The Room:** _____

# NOTES

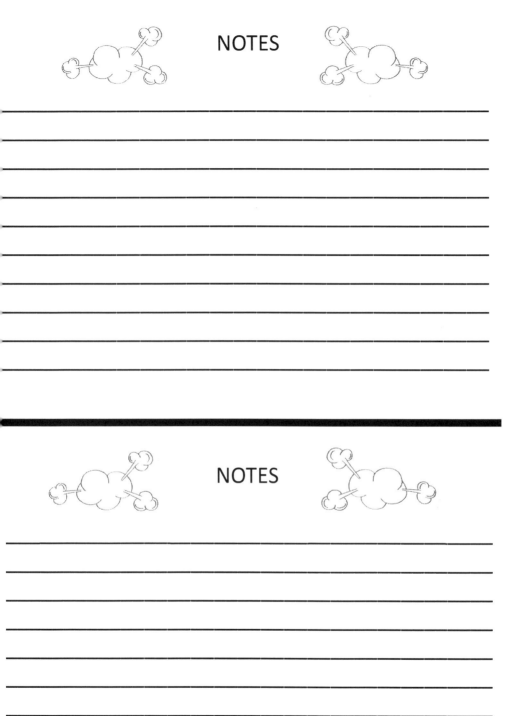

# NOTES

**Date:** ___ / ___ / ___     Sun  Mon  Tue  Wed  Thu  Fri  Sat

**Time of Fart:** _____ am/pm     **Duration:** ___ min ___ sec

**Fart Intensity:**
- ○ **Gentle Puff** (barely there, quick & unscented)
- ○ **SBD** (silent but deadly)
- ○ **Military March** (series of puffs with mild scent)
- ○ **Classic** (quick, loud, stinky scent but fades quickly)
- ○ **Thunder Rumble** (long, loud & stinky)
- ○ **Diarrhea Storm** (explosive, wet & clears the room)
- ○ **Oh, Crap!** (self explanatory)

**Fart Enjoyment Scale:**  ☺ ☺ ☺ ☺ ☺

**Who Noticed:** _____

**Who Left The Room:** _____

---

**Date:** ___ / ___ / ___     Sun  Mon  Tue  Wed  Thu  Fri  Sat

**Time of Fart:** _____ am/pm     **Duration:** ___ min ___ sec

**Fart Intensity:**
- ○ **Gentle Puff** (barely there, quick & unscented)
- ○ **SBD** (silent but deadly)
- ○ **Military March** (series of puffs with mild scent)
- ○ **Classic** (quick, loud, stinky scent but fades quickly)
- ○ **Thunder Rumble** (long, loud & stinky)
- ○ **Diarrhea Storm** (explosive, wet & clears the room)
- ○ **Oh, Crap!** (self explanatory)

**Fart Enjoyment Scale:**  ☺ ☺ ☺ ☺ ☺

**Who Noticed:** _____

**Who Left The Room:** _____

# NOTES

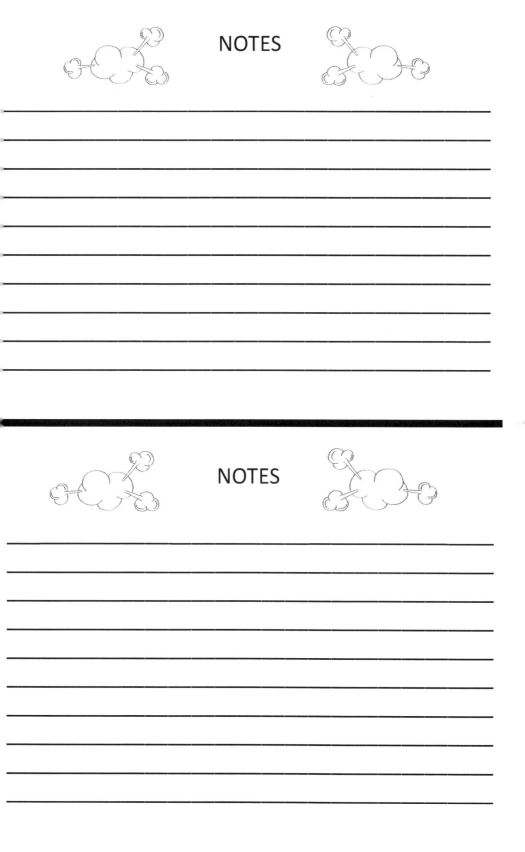

# NOTES

**Date:** ___ / ___ / ___     Sun  Mon  Tue  Wed  Thu  Fri  Sat

**Time of Fart:** _____ am/pm    **Duration:** ____ min ____ sec

**Fart Intensity:**
- ○ **Gentle Puff** (barely there, quick & unscented)
- ○ **SBD** (silent but deadly)
- ○ **Military March** (series of puffs with mild scent)
- ○ **Classic** (quick, loud, stinky scent but fades quickly)
- ○ **Thunder Rumble** (long, loud & stinky)
- ○ **Diarrhea Storm** (explosive, wet & clears the room)
- ○ **Oh, Crap!** (self explanatory)

**Fart Enjoyment Scale:** ☺ ☺ ☺ ☺ ☺

**Who Noticed:** _____

**Who Left The Room:** _____

---

**Date:** ___ / ___ / ___     Sun  Mon  Tue  Wed  Thu  Fri  Sat

**Time of Fart:** _____ am/pm    **Duration:** ____ min ____ sec

**Fart Intensity:**
- ○ **Gentle Puff** (barely there, quick & unscented)
- ○ **SBD** (silent but deadly)
- ○ **Military March** (series of puffs with mild scent)
- ○ **Classic** (quick, loud, stinky scent but fades quickly)
- ○ **Thunder Rumble** (long, loud & stinky)
- ○ **Diarrhea Storm** (explosive, wet & clears the room)
- ○ **Oh, Crap!** (self explanatory)

**Fart Enjoyment Scale:** ☺ ☺ ☺ ☺ ☺

**Who Noticed:** _____

**Who Left The Room:** _____

# NOTES

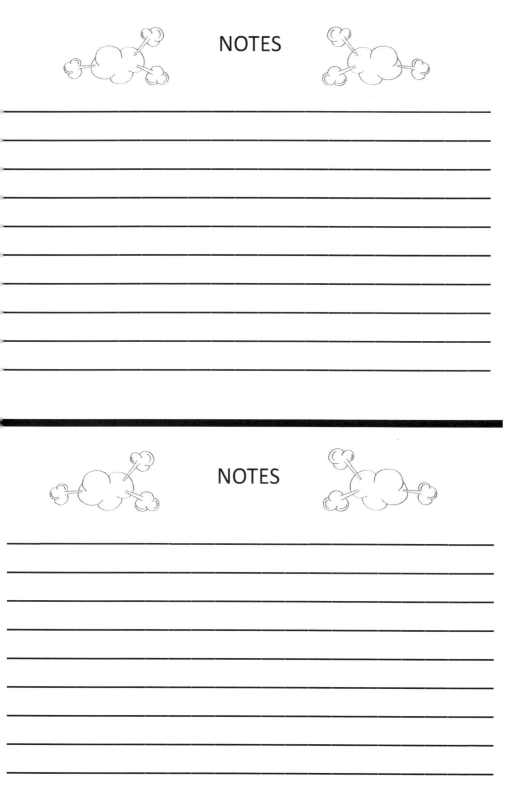

# NOTES

**Date:** ___ / ___ / ___      Sun  Mon  Tue  Wed  Thu  Fri  Sat

**Time of Fart:** _____ am/pm      **Duration:** ___ min ___ sec

**Fart Intensity:**
- ○ **Gentle Puff** (barely there, quick & unscented)
- ○ **SBD** (silent but deadly)
- ○ **Military March** (series of puffs with mild scent)
- ○ **Classic** (quick, loud, stinky scent but fades quickly)
- ○ **Thunder Rumble** (long, loud & stinky)
- ○ **Diarrhea Storm** (explosive, wet & clears the room)
- ○ **Oh, Crap!** (self explanatory)

**Fart Enjoyment Scale:** ☺ ☺ ☺ ☺ ☺

**Who Noticed:** _____

**Who Left The Room:** _____

---

**Date:** ___ / ___ / ___      Sun  Mon  Tue  Wed  Thu  Fri  Sat

**Time of Fart:** _____ am/pm      **Duration:** ___ min ___ sec

**Fart Intensity:**
- ○ **Gentle Puff** (barely there, quick & unscented)
- ○ **SBD** (silent but deadly)
- ○ **Military March** (series of puffs with mild scent)
- ○ **Classic** (quick, loud, stinky scent but fades quickly)
- ○ **Thunder Rumble** (long, loud & stinky)
- ○ **Diarrhea Storm** (explosive, wet & clears the room)
- ○ **Oh, Crap!** (self explanatory)

**Fart Enjoyment Scale:** ☺ ☺ ☺ ☺ ☺

**Who Noticed:** _____

**Who Left The Room:** _____

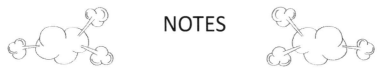

# NOTES

_____
_____
_____
_____
_____
_____
_____
_____
_____
_____
_____
_____

# NOTES

_____
_____
_____
_____
_____
_____
_____
_____
_____
_____
_____

**Date:** ___ / ___ / ___   Sun  Mon  Tue  Wed  Thu  Fri  Sat

**Time of Fart:** _____ am/pm   **Duration:** ___ min ___ sec

**Fart Intensity:**
- ○ **Gentle Puff** (barely there, quick & unscented)
- ○ **SBD** (silent but deadly)
- ○ **Military March** (series of puffs with mild scent)
- ○ **Classic** (quick, loud, stinky scent but fades quickly)
- ○ **Thunder Rumble** (long, loud & stinky)
- ○ **Diarrhea Storm** (explosive, wet & clears the room)
- ○ **Oh, Crap!** (self explanatory)

**Fart Enjoyment Scale:**  ☺ ☺ ☺ ☺ ☺

**Who Noticed:** _____

**Who Left The Room:** _____

---

**Date:** ___ / ___ / ___   Sun  Mon  Tue  Wed  Thu  Fri  Sat

**Time of Fart:** _____ am/pm   **Duration:** ___ min ___ sec

**Fart Intensity:**
- ○ **Gentle Puff** (barely there, quick & unscented)
- ○ **SBD** (silent but deadly)
- ○ **Military March** (series of puffs with mild scent)
- ○ **Classic** (quick, loud, stinky scent but fades quickly)
- ○ **Thunder Rumble** (long, loud & stinky)
- ○ **Diarrhea Storm** (explosive, wet & clears the room)
- ○ **Oh, Crap!** (self explanatory)

**Fart Enjoyment Scale:**  ☺ ☺ ☺ ☺ ☺

**Who Noticed:** _____

**Who Left The Room:** _____

# NOTES

---

# NOTES

**Date:** ___ / ___ / ___     Sun  Mon  Tue  Wed  Thu  Fri  Sat

**Time of Fart:** _____ am/pm     **Duration:** ___ min ___ sec

**Fart Intensity:**
- ○ **Gentle Puff** (barely there, quick & unscented)
- ○ **SBD** (silent but deadly)
- ○ **Military March** (series of puffs with mild scent)
- ○ **Classic** (quick, loud, stinky scent but fades quickly)
- ○ **Thunder Rumble** (long, loud & stinky)
- ○ **Diarrhea Storm** (explosive, wet & clears the room)
- ○ **Oh, Crap!** (self explanatory)

**Fart Enjoyment Scale:**  ☺ ☺ ☺ ☺ ☺

**Who Noticed:** _____

**Who Left The Room:** _____

---

**Date:** ___ / ___ / ___     Sun  Mon  Tue  Wed  Thu  Fri  Sat

**Time of Fart:** _____ am/pm     **Duration:** ___ min ___ sec

**Fart Intensity:**
- ○ **Gentle Puff** (barely there, quick & unscented)
- ○ **SBD** (silent but deadly)
- ○ **Military March** (series of puffs with mild scent)
- ○ **Classic** (quick, loud, stinky scent but fades quickly)
- ○ **Thunder Rumble** (long, loud & stinky)
- ○ **Diarrhea Storm** (explosive, wet & clears the room)
- ○ **Oh, Crap!** (self explanatory)

**Fart Enjoyment Scale:**  ☺ ☺ ☺ ☺ ☺

**Who Noticed:** _____

**Who Left The Room:** _____

# NOTES

# NOTES

**Date:** ___ / ___ / ___     Sun  Mon  Tue  Wed  Thu  Fri  Sat

**Time of Fart:** _____ am/pm     **Duration:** ___ min ___ sec

**Fart Intensity:**
- ○ **Gentle Puff** (barely there, quick & unscented)
- ○ **SBD** (silent but deadly)
- ○ **Military March** (series of puffs with mild scent)
- ○ **Classic** (quick, loud, stinky scent but fades quickly)
- ○ **Thunder Rumble** (long, loud & stinky)
- ○ **Diarrhea Storm** (explosive, wet & clears the room)
- ○ **Oh, Crap!** (self explanatory)

**Fart Enjoyment Scale:**  😊  😊  😊  😊  😊

**Who Noticed:** _____

**Who Left The Room:** _____

---

**Date:** ___ / ___ / ___     Sun  Mon  Tue  Wed  Thu  Fri  Sat

**Time of Fart:** _____ am/pm     **Duration:** ___ min ___ sec

**Fart Intensity:**
- ○ **Gentle Puff** (barely there, quick & unscented)
- ○ **SBD** (silent but deadly)
- ○ **Military March** (series of puffs with mild scent)
- ○ **Classic** (quick, loud, stinky scent but fades quickly)
- ○ **Thunder Rumble** (long, loud & stinky)
- ○ **Diarrhea Storm** (explosive, wet & clears the room)
- ○ **Oh, Crap!** (self explanatory)

**Fart Enjoyment Scale:**  😊  😊  😊  😊  😊

**Who Noticed:** _____

**Who Left The Room:** _____

# NOTES

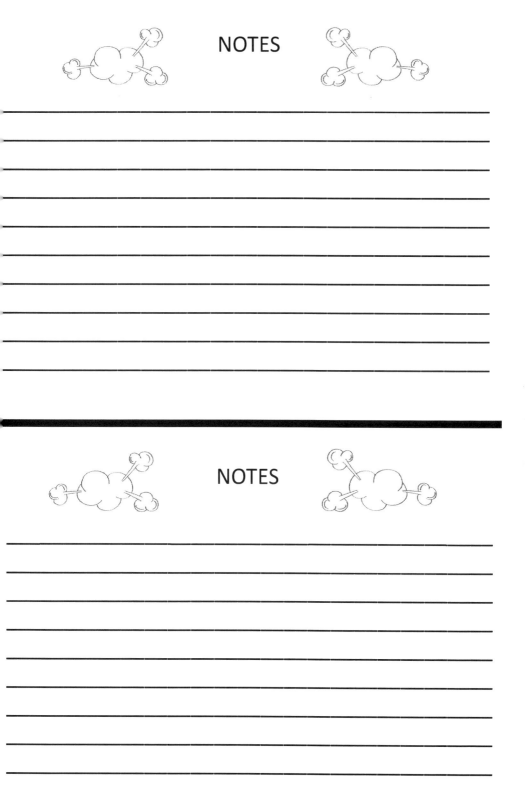

# NOTES

**Date:** ___ / ___ / ___    Sun  Mon  Tue  Wed  Thu  Fri  Sat

**Time of Fart:** _____ am/pm    **Duration:** ____ min ____ sec

**Fart Intensity:**
- ○ **Gentle Puff** (barely there, quick & unscented)
- ○ **SBD** (silent but deadly)
- ○ **Military March** (series of puffs with mild scent)
- ○ **Classic** (quick, loud, stinky scent but fades quickly)
- ○ **Thunder Rumble** (long, loud & stinky)
- ○ **Diarrhea Storm** (explosive, wet & clears the room)
- ○ **Oh, Crap!** (self explanatory)

**Fart Enjoyment Scale:** ☺ ☺ ☺ ☺ ☺

**Who Noticed:** _____

**Who Left The Room:** _____

---

**Date:** ___ / ___ / ___    Sun  Mon  Tue  Wed  Thu  Fri  Sat

**Time of Fart:** _____ am/pm    **Duration:** ____ min ____ sec

**Fart Intensity:**
- ○ **Gentle Puff** (barely there, quick & unscented)
- ○ **SBD** (silent but deadly)
- ○ **Military March** (series of puffs with mild scent)
- ○ **Classic** (quick, loud, stinky scent but fades quickly)
- ○ **Thunder Rumble** (long, loud & stinky)
- ○ **Diarrhea Storm** (explosive, wet & clears the room)
- ○ **Oh, Crap!** (self explanatory)

**Fart Enjoyment Scale:** ☺ ☺ ☺ ☺ ☺

**Who Noticed:** _____

**Who Left The Room:** _____

# NOTES

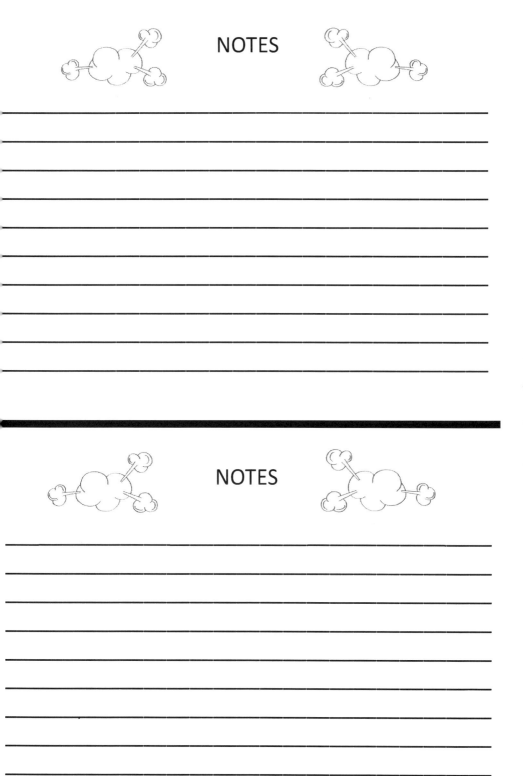

# NOTES

**Date:** ___ / ___ / ___     Sun   Mon   Tue   Wed   Thu   Fri   Sat

**Time of Fart:** _____ am/pm     **Duration:** ___ min ___ sec

**Fart Intensity:**
- ○ **Gentle Puff** (barely there, quick & unscented)
- ○ **SBD** (silent but deadly)
- ○ **Military March** (series of puffs with mild scent)
- ○ **Classic** (quick, loud, stinky scent but fades quickly)
- ○ **Thunder Rumble** (long, loud & stinky)
- ○ **Diarrhea Storm** (explosive, wet & clears the room)
- ○ **Oh, Crap!** (self explanatory)

**Fart Enjoyment Scale:** ☺ ☺ ☺ ☺ ☺

**Who Noticed:** _____

**Who Left The Room:** _____

---

**Date:** ___ / ___ / ___     Sun   Mon   Tue   Wed   Thu   Fri   Sat

**Time of Fart:** _____ am/pm     **Duration:** ___ min ___ sec

**Fart Intensity:**
- ○ **Gentle Puff** (barely there, quick & unscented)
- ○ **SBD** (silent but deadly)
- ○ **Military March** (series of puffs with mild scent)
- ○ **Classic** (quick, loud, stinky scent but fades quickly)
- ○ **Thunder Rumble** (long, loud & stinky)
- ○ **Diarrhea Storm** (explosive, wet & clears the room)
- ○ **Oh, Crap!** (self explanatory)

**Fart Enjoyment Scale:** ☺ ☺ ☺ ☺ ☺

**Who Noticed:** _____

**Who Left The Room:** _____

# NOTES

_____

_____

_____

_____

_____

_____

_____

_____

_____

_____

_____

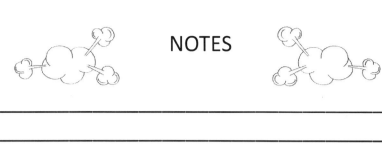

# NOTES

_____

_____

_____

_____

_____

_____

_____

_____

_____

**Date:** ___ / ___ / ___    Sun  Mon  Tue  Wed  Thu  Fri  Sat

**Time of Fart:** _____ am/pm    **Duration:** ___ min ___ sec

**Fart Intensity:**
- ○ **Gentle Puff** (barely there, quick & unscented)
- ○ **SBD** (silent but deadly)
- ○ **Military March** (series of puffs with mild scent)
- ○ **Classic** (quick, loud, stinky scent but fades quickly)
- ○ **Thunder Rumble** (long, loud & stinky)
- ○ **Diarrhea Storm** (explosive, wet & clears the room)
- ○ **Oh, Crap!** (self explanatory)

**Fart Enjoyment Scale:**  ☺ ☺ ☺ ☺ ☺

**Who Noticed:** _____

**Who Left The Room:** _____

---

**Date:** ___ / ___ / ___    Sun  Mon  Tue  Wed  Thu  Fri  Sat

**Time of Fart:** _____ am/pm    **Duration:** ___ min ___ sec

**Fart Intensity:**
- ○ **Gentle Puff** (barely there, quick & unscented)
- ○ **SBD** (silent but deadly)
- ○ **Military March** (series of puffs with mild scent)
- ○ **Classic** (quick, loud, stinky scent but fades quickly)
- ○ **Thunder Rumble** (long, loud & stinky)
- ○ **Diarrhea Storm** (explosive, wet & clears the room)
- ○ **Oh, Crap!** (self explanatory)

**Fart Enjoyment Scale:**  ☺ ☺ ☺ ☺ ☺

**Who Noticed:** _____

**Who Left The Room:** _____

# NOTES

_____
_____
_____
_____
_____
_____
_____
_____
_____
_____
_____
_____

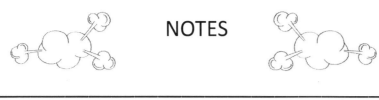

# NOTES

_____
_____
_____
_____
_____
_____
_____
_____
_____
_____

**Date:** ___ / ___ / ___     Sun  Mon  Tue  Wed  Thu  Fri  Sat

**Time of Fart:** _____ am/pm     **Duration:** ____ min ____ sec

**Fart Intensity:**
- ○ **Gentle Puff** (barely there, quick & unscented)
- ○ **SBD** (silent but deadly)
- ○ **Military March** (series of puffs with mild scent)
- ○ **Classic** (quick, loud, stinky scent but fades quickly)
- ○ **Thunder Rumble** (long, loud & stinky)
- ○ **Diarrhea Storm** (explosive, wet & clears the room)
- ○ **Oh, Crap!** (self explanatory)

**Fart Enjoyment Scale:**  ☺ ☺ ☺ ☺ ☺

**Who Noticed:** _____

**Who Left The Room:** _____

---

**Date:** ___ / ___ / ___     Sun  Mon  Tue  Wed  Thu  Fri  Sat

**Time of Fart:** _____ am/pm     **Duration:** ____ min ____ sec

**Fart Intensity:**
- ○ **Gentle Puff** (barely there, quick & unscented)
- ○ **SBD** (silent but deadly)
- ○ **Military March** (series of puffs with mild scent)
- ○ **Classic** (quick, loud, stinky scent but fades quickly)
- ○ **Thunder Rumble** (long, loud & stinky)
- ○ **Diarrhea Storm** (explosive, wet & clears the room)
- ○ **Oh, Crap!** (self explanatory)

**Fart Enjoyment Scale:**  ☺ ☺ ☺ ☺ ☺

**Who Noticed:** _____

**Who Left The Room:** _____

# NOTES

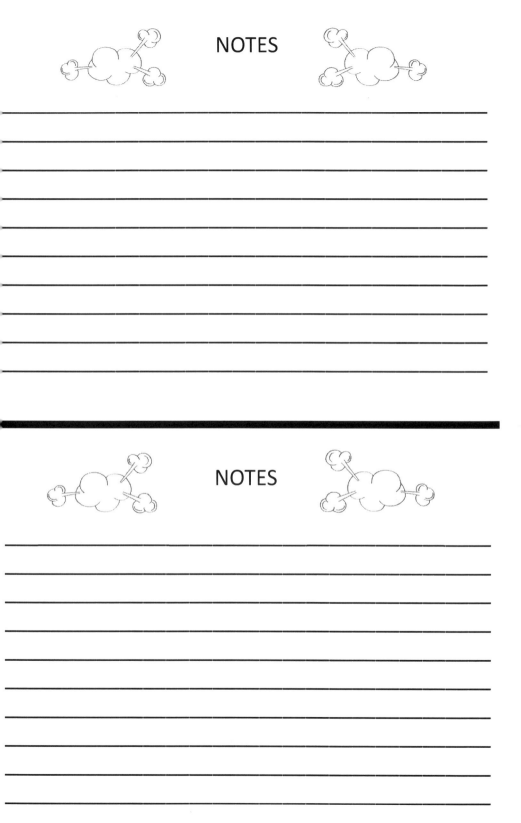

# NOTES

**Date:** ___ / ___ / ___     Sun  Mon  Tue  Wed  Thu  Fri  Sat

**Time of Fart:** _____ am/pm     **Duration:** ___ min ___ sec

**Fart Intensity:**
- ○ **Gentle Puff** (barely there, quick & unscented)
- ○ **SBD** (silent but deadly)
- ○ **Military March** (series of puffs with mild scent)
- ○ **Classic** (quick, loud, stinky scent but fades quickly)
- ○ **Thunder Rumble** (long, loud & stinky)
- ○ **Diarrhea Storm** (explosive, wet & clears the room)
- ○ **Oh, Crap!** (self explanatory)

**Fart Enjoyment Scale:**   ☺  ☺  ☺  ☺  ☺

**Who Noticed:** _____

**Who Left The Room:** _____

---

**Date:** ___ / ___ / ___     Sun  Mon  Tue  Wed  Thu  Fri  Sat

**Time of Fart:** _____ am/pm     **Duration:** ___ min ___ sec

**Fart Intensity:**
- ○ **Gentle Puff** (barely there, quick & unscented)
- ○ **SBD** (silent but deadly)
- ○ **Military March** (series of puffs with mild scent)
- ○ **Classic** (quick, loud, stinky scent but fades quickly)
- ○ **Thunder Rumble** (long, loud & stinky)
- ○ **Diarrhea Storm** (explosive, wet & clears the room)
- ○ **Oh, Crap!** (self explanatory)

**Fart Enjoyment Scale:**   ☺  ☺  ☺  ☺  ☺

**Who Noticed:** _____

**Who Left The Room:** _____

# NOTES

# NOTES

**Date:** ___ / ___ / ___     Sun   Mon   Tue   Wed   Thu   Fri   Sat

**Time of Fart:** _____ am/pm     **Duration:** ___ min ___ sec

**Fart Intensity:**
- ○ **Gentle Puff** (barely there, quick & unscented)
- ○ **SBD** (silent but deadly)
- ○ **Military March** (series of puffs with mild scent)
- ○ **Classic** (quick, loud, stinky scent but fades quickly)
- ○ **Thunder Rumble** (long, loud & stinky)
- ○ **Diarrhea Storm** (explosive, wet & clears the room)
- ○ **Oh, Crap!** (self explanatory)

**Fart Enjoyment Scale:**   ☺ ☺ ☺ ☺ ☺

**Who Noticed:** _____

**Who Left The Room:** _____

---

**Date:** ___ / ___ / ___     Sun   Mon   Tue   Wed   Thu   Fri   Sat

**Time of Fart:** _____ am/pm     **Duration:** ___ min ___ sec

**Fart Intensity:**
- ○ **Gentle Puff** (barely there, quick & unscented)
- ○ **SBD** (silent but deadly)
- ○ **Military March** (series of puffs with mild scent)
- ○ **Classic** (quick, loud, stinky scent but fades quickly)
- ○ **Thunder Rumble** (long, loud & stinky)
- ○ **Diarrhea Storm** (explosive, wet & clears the room)
- ○ **Oh, Crap!** (self explanatory)

**Fart Enjoyment Scale:**   ☺ ☺ ☺ ☺ ☺

**Who Noticed:** _____

**Who Left The Room:** _____

# NOTES

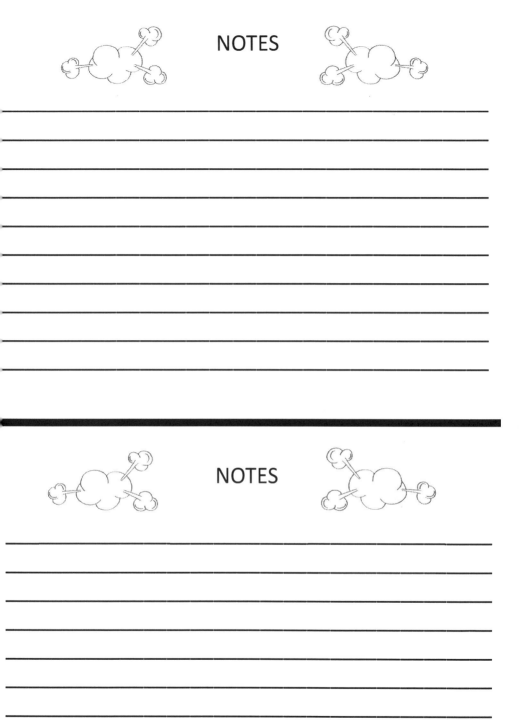

# NOTES

**Date:** ___ / ___ / ___    Sun  Mon  Tue  Wed  Thu  Fri  Sat

**Time of Fart:** _____ am/pm    **Duration:** ___ min ___ sec

**Fart Intensity:**
- ○ **Gentle Puff** (barely there, quick & unscented)
- ○ **SBD** (silent but deadly)
- ○ **Military March** (series of puffs with mild scent)
- ○ **Classic** (quick, loud, stinky scent but fades quickly)
- ○ **Thunder Rumble** (long, loud & stinky)
- ○ **Diarrhea Storm** (explosive, wet & clears the room)
- ○ **Oh, Crap!** (self explanatory)

**Fart Enjoyment Scale:** ☺ ☺ ☺ ☺ ☺

**Who Noticed:** _____

**Who Left The Room:** _____

---

**Date:** ___ / ___ / ___    Sun  Mon  Tue  Wed  Thu  Fri  Sat

**Time of Fart:** _____ am/pm    **Duration:** ___ min ___ sec

**Fart Intensity:**
- ○ **Gentle Puff** (barely there, quick & unscented)
- ○ **SBD** (silent but deadly)
- ○ **Military March** (series of puffs with mild scent)
- ○ **Classic** (quick, loud, stinky scent but fades quickly)
- ○ **Thunder Rumble** (long, loud & stinky)
- ○ **Diarrhea Storm** (explosive, wet & clears the room)
- ○ **Oh, Crap!** (self explanatory)

**Fart Enjoyment Scale:** ☺ ☺ ☺ ☺ ☺

**Who Noticed:** _____

**Who Left The Room:** _____

# NOTES

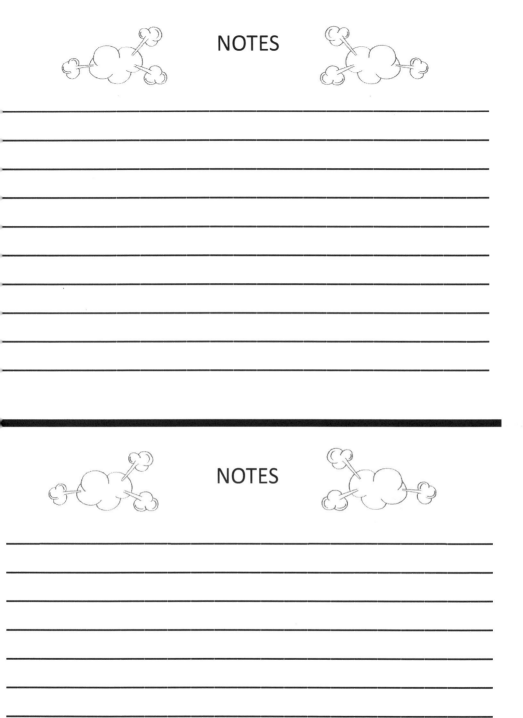

# NOTES

**Date:** ___ / ___ / ___     Sun  Mon  Tue  Wed  Thu  Fri  Sat

**Time of Fart:** _____ am/pm     **Duration:** ___ min ___ sec

**Fart Intensity:**
- ○ **Gentle Puff** (barely there, quick & unscented)
- ○ **SBD** (silent but deadly)
- ○ **Military March** (series of puffs with mild scent)
- ○ **Classic** (quick, loud, stinky scent but fades quickly)
- ○ **Thunder Rumble** (long, loud & stinky)
- ○ **Diarrhea Storm** (explosive, wet & clears the room)
- ○ **Oh, Crap!** (self explanatory)

**Fart Enjoyment Scale:**  ☺ ☺ ☺ ☺ ☺

**Who Noticed:** _____

**Who Left The Room:** _____

---

**Date:** ___ / ___ / ___     Sun  Mon  Tue  Wed  Thu  Fri  Sat

**Time of Fart:** _____ am/pm     **Duration:** ___ min ___ sec

**Fart Intensity:**
- ○ **Gentle Puff** (barely there, quick & unscented)
- ○ **SBD** (silent but deadly)
- ○ **Military March** (series of puffs with mild scent)
- ○ **Classic** (quick, loud, stinky scent but fades quickly)
- ○ **Thunder Rumble** (long, loud & stinky)
- ○ **Diarrhea Storm** (explosive, wet & clears the room)
- ○ **Oh, Crap!** (self explanatory)

**Fart Enjoyment Scale:**  ☺ ☺ ☺ ☺ ☺

**Who Noticed:** _____

**Who Left The Room:** _____

Printed in Great
Britain
by Amazon